Princeton Theologi

Dikran Y. Hadidian

General Editor

32

AMBUSHED BY GRACE

THE VIRTUES OF A USELESS FAITH

THOMAS W. CURRIE III

AMBUSHED

BY

GRACE

THE VIRTUES OF A USELESS FAITH

PICKWICK PUBLICATIONS
ALLISON PARK, PENNSYLVANIA

Published by

Pickwick Publications
4137 Timberlane Drive
Allison Park, PA 15101-2932

Printed in the United States of America

Library of Congress Cataloging-in-Publication Data

Currie, Thomas W.
    Ambushed by Grace : the virtues of a useless faith / Thomas W.
Currie, III.
      p. cm. -- (Princeton theological monograph series ; 32)
    Includes bibliographical references.
    ISBN 1-55635-017-1
    1. Freedom (Theology) 2. Grace (Theology) 3. Faith.
4. Christianity and culture--Controversial literature.
5. Relevance. I. Title. II. Series.
BT810.2.C84 1993
230--dc20   93-2701
                                            CIP

This book
is dedicated to my wife,

PEGGY DAVENPORT CURRIE

CONTENTS

ACKNOWLEDGEMENTS

This little book grew out of a conversation I had about four years ago with the Rev. John B. Rogers, pastor of First Presbyterian Church, Shreveport, Louisiana. For better or for worse, he encouraged me to write and then was gracious enough to read what I had written. Though he in no way should be blamed for the book's faults, or even its point of view, he did provide much of the initial stimulus for my own effort to think through these matters. His example in the ministry, his deep love for the church, his good sense and eloquence in the pulpit and at the lectern, and his warmth and generosity of spirit have continued to inspire me and in any case, deserve more than the simple acknowledgement accorded here.

The first three chapters were written at the Bridwell Library of Perkins School of Theology at Southern Methodist University. I wish to thank my sister, Liz Williams, for directing my path to the doors of that institution. And I would like to thank my parents for hosting me while I was staying in Dallas and for reading parts of the manuscript as it developed.

In an earlier form, the first three chapters were read by Dr. George S. Heyer and Dr. Robert M. Shelton, both of whom teach at Austin Presbyterian Theological Seminary. I have benefited, I believe, from their comments and am grateful to them for their willingness to share those comments with me. I also wish to express my deepest appreciation to another member of Austin Seminary's staff, Mrs. Genevieve R. Luna, Assistant Librarian for Circulation and Reader Services at the Stitt Library, who deftly tracked down some elusive quotations for me.

In addition, I wish to thank the St. Giles Presbyterian Church of Houston and the First Presbyterian Church of Camden, Arkansas for inviting me to share, in a lecture format, the substance of this book with them. Their hospitality and grace, their joy in struggling with matters of the faith, their vigorous dissents and happy affirmations combined to renew my spirit and to remind me once again of the singular blessing of life together as the church of Jesus Christ. That blessing is one that is mediated to me daily through the life of First Presbyterian Church, Kerrville, whose patience with me while I labored to give birth to this book is also deeply appreciated.

Finally, I wish to thank my colleague and friend, Mrs. Nancy Wilbourn, whose close attention to the final copy of the manuscript improved its appearance considerably. Having eliminated so many of my own errors in spelling, grammar and punctuation, she did her best to save me from further embarrassment. That which remains, however, is entirely my own.

Thomas W. Currie
Epiphany 1993

INTRODUCTION

The Uselessness Of Faith

The dilemma the church faces today can be sum-
marized as follows: the church is called upon to believe in
Jesus Christ and the power of his resurrection; what it
wants, however, is to be useful.

At first glance, this dilemma might not appear to be
real. After all, does not the church give evidence of its usefulness insofar as it witnesses to Jesus Christ and proclaims
in its life and work the power of his resurrection? No doubt.
But the question soon arises as to the goal of that usefulness: useful to whom, for example, and how? Over time,
the church has learned how to be useful to more than one
master. Constantine, for example, found the church's witness useful in organizing his empire, providing, as it did,
the religious glue that promised to hold that political structure together. Or to take another quite different example,
Paul Tillich found the Christian faith useful in answering
the "ultimate concerns" of a secularized culture, a culture
which, in turn, could make use of a therapeutic faith. Or to
take yet even another example, some parts of the church
find the gospel of salvation useful today for the liberation
of certain oppressive political regimes, while other parts of
the church find that same gospel useful for the liberation of
personal guilt and private demons; yet, in both instances, it
is the salvific usefulness of the gospel that is both prized
and honored. What counts is the way in which the gospel
transforms the culture and rearranges its power structure;
what matters is the way in which the gospel triumphs over
my sin and guilt and saves me from their imprisoning pow-

er. But, in all cases, what recommends the gospel is its usefulness to a culture that has perceived quite well its own needs and finds in the gospel a remedy or therapy of redemption.

To argue then, as I will, that the fruitfulness of the church's witness depends on its discovering or, better, rediscovering its own uselessness may strike some as quixotic at best, an argument for doing nothing at worst. Faith, however, often looks irresponsible in the eyes of a culture which is out to preserve itself; indeed, in such a culture faith is always going to be invited to dispense with its listening to Jesus, and to distract itself with much serving. That that is precisely the position of the church today is the burden of this little book. "One thing is needful," Jesus says, and that is a faith in him that simply attends to his presence, a faith that does not follow him in order to be useful or saved or liberated but rejoices in him for the sake of life together in him. It is that joy that our so very useful faith lacks today, and it is that joy that alone is the true promise of the gospel and the true life of the church. If the redeemed of the Lord don't look it, it may be because they have made themselves useful. Salvation, on the other hand, Luther reminds us, means *forgetting* self, even forgetting how useful the faith is in justifying our various programs of redemption. The church is drowning in usefulness; the culture is happy to receive the gospel as therapy or strategy for this or that project, especially if it means not having to receive it as *gospel*. What is missing is the "one thing needful," the attending to Jesus Christ, the *being* of his church as the meaning of his ministry. That joy, that cost, that pilgrimage we have lost. Instead we have become . . . busy.

Simone Weil in her book *Waiting For God,* claims that she never sought for God, that, in fact, she never really liked that expression.[1] "Searching . . . leads only to error; obedience is the sole way to truth."[2] The role of the church is to wait, as a husband or wife awaits the spouse. And yet such a waiting is anything but quietistic, or at least no more so than was Weil's own life. It is a waiting in obedience, an action in waiting, but, nevertheless, a waiting and a hungering for someone in particular, and so a waiting that is always clear about what is important and what is not, a waiting that does not have to dream up ways to "kill time" but, instead, redeems the time in obedience to the coming Lord. In this sense, Mary is the true exemplar of the church, as over against Martha, even though all Mary does is wait. She waits on Jesus; she listens; she attends. There will be time for serving, but serving can be the enemy of obedience as well as its instrument. Mary chooses Jesus, chooses Jesus even over service and, in doing so, becomes the church. Indeed, in doing so, Mary witnesses to the *freedom* of the church to be the church in opposition to all the world's definitions of usefulness. Mary does not do a single useful thing. Martha is right. She neither serves nor helps to clean up. She neither feeds the hungry nor clothes the naked. All she does is listen, an activity which, from the culture's point of view, even from the point of view of religion, does no one any good. She is useless. Yet precisely in such uselessness is her freedom for God revealed.

      The argument of this book pivots on that notion of Freedom, the Freedom of the church to be the church, to rejoice in the divine comedy of the gospel, over against the all too serious therapies of self-realization thrown up by the culture. That freedom is rooted in the freedom of Jesus Christ, which, in turn, is the incarnation of the freedom of God's triune being. To a culture bent on merely using the faith, such talk of freedom makes no sense; indeed, such freedom seems utterly useless. A church that is free will always be useless to a culture trying to realize itself; a Savior who offers only himself will always seem useless to a culture which wants salvation as a therapy and not as a person; a God who names himself will always appear useless to a culture that only wants a God that it can name, whether that be a goddess or the political idols of race or ideology. And yet, such uselessness, such freedom, is precisely what the church has to offer the world. The sadness of it all is not that the world often finds such uselessness baffling but that the church itself does not trust its own gift; rather, it is all too ready to jettison its freedom in order to render itself useful to the world.

Accordingly, I will try to outline in four chapters
the dimensions of the church's saving uselessness in the
hope that the church might rediscover the gift it has to give
the world, that is, that the church might understand its own
life as the gift of freedom. Such freedom is clearly bound
up with the freedom of Jesus Christ, and therefore the first
chapter deals with the "useless Savior," who, in refusing to
define his ministry in terms of its usefulness to the world,
overcomes salvation as the primary goal of the Christian
life. The fact is that Jesus makes a poor Savior, or even
"Liberator", for that matter, since his gospel makes it incon-
veniently clear that the cross stands athwart any plans Jesus
might have had to save himself. If achieving his own salvation is not the goal of his life, how can it be the goal of the
Christian life? (It is a sign of how deeply corrupt our own
theologizing has become that we all too easily assume that
the chief end of God is the salvation of humankind, an assumption that is plainly idolatrous.) What the cross suggests is, rather, that the goal of Christ's life is to be found in
his freely choosing to obey his Father's will, a choosing
which places him in inseparable solidarity with sinners,
such that he clearly refuses any salvation that would save
him apart from them, even in the end choosing the death
that is their lot in order to incorporate them into his life.
Salvation in this sense then is not to "get somewhere" so
much as it is to be wherever Christ is, i.e., to be in union
with him, and in him to discover our own solidarity with
sinners of every sort, learning of that from him who "was
made to be sin" for us (2 Cor. 5.21).

But to speak of Jesus Christ's uselessness is really to
speak of his freedom, a freedom that is rooted in the freedom of his being God with us. Therefore, the second chapter attempts to locate that freedom within the triune being
of God. The church, I will argue, understands and affirms
its own freedom to the extent that it understands and affirms the significance of the doctrine of the Trinity. To the
extent that the church does not see in this doctrine anything
of constitutive significance, to that extent does the church

lose its own freedom and become acculturated to the world. The doctrine of the Trinity, as a description of God's redemptive uselessness, is, then, the church's effort to witness to the freedom of God and is a primary indication that salvation is not the end of the Christian story but, rather, only a subordinate part which is given its appropriate (and, to be sure, important) place in the triumph of the glory of God.

The triumph of God in Jesus Christ over all that threatens to destroy his loving purpose creates space for the church. Indeed, that the church cannot be understood except in the light of Jesus Christ might seem a commonplace today were it not for the fact that the church is interpreted in every light but this one. Hence, its usefulness. The fact that the church is as mysteriously useless as its redemptive Lord is difficult for us to swallow, especially for those of us committed to rendering the church useful as a therapy or technology of redemption. The third chapter, then, will deal with the uselessness of the church and will attempt to construe the Christian life as worship and witness.

Finally, there is preaching. It is not obvious that the preaching task belongs to this discussion. One might well conclude in another fashion, perhaps with a discussion of ethics or even the educational task of the church. But the freedom of the church will not be seen in all its scandal, as the freedom of Jesus Christ, unless the uselessness of preaching is discerned and even celebrated. "For the word of the cross is folly to those who are perishing, but to us who are being saved, it is the power of God." (1Cor.1:18) And it is the power of God, not because we are being saved but because it is the word of the cross that can overcome even our perishing usefulness and make salvation itself render the praise of God.

NOTES

1. Simone Weil, *Waiting for God,* trans. Emma Craufurd,

(New York: Perennial Library, 1973), p. 62 "I may say that never at
any moment in my life have I 'sought for God'."
    2. *Ibid.* p. 28.

The Uselessness of Jesus Christ:
Overcoming Salvation as
the End of the Christian Life

Nothing seems more at odds with the church's proclamation today than to suggest that Jesus Christ is useless. He is, after all, our Savior. He is the first-born of the marginalized, the liberator of the oppressed, the personal Savior of the lost sinner. It is clear that the church has found and continues to find him enormously useful.

How strange it is, then, that Jesus, at least in the gospel narratives, rejects again and again the useful roles proffered to him, choosing in the end what by all accounts was the most useless role of all, namely, death.

Consider, for example, the beginning of Jesus' ministry in Luke's gospel. There, as in Matthew and Mark, Jesus is led by the Spirit into the wilderness to be tested by the devil. What is the nature of this test? The test concerns whether or not Jesus will be willing to play a useful role in the society of his day, helping it, in fact, to organize itself into a more humane and compassionate world. This test takes the form of rendering faith useful to the culture, that is, making it serve some other (praiseworthy) goal, i.e., feeding the world, establishing world peace, even bringing salvation. The alternative Jesus chooses in all three instances is not only one that is revealed in Scripture as placing faith in the exclusive service of God, but also one that claims that true human freedom is rooted only in the freedom to be free for God. Clearly, though, this claim renders

him useless to a culture possessing not only its own idea of
human freedom but also its own idea of salvation. Indeed,
in Luke's gospel, the end of the story comes when Jesus finally even rejects salvation as the chief goal of the Christian life. His ministry can only begin when that temptation
is put aside, but once it has been rejected, then Jesus can
truly begin his long journey to the cross and to freedom.

So how does the story of Jesus' useless freedom unfold? It begins with the devil's pointing out a rather obvious
fact: we do not live in a perfect world. In fact, we live in a
world full of starvation, hunger, and death. Jesus himself,
fasting as if he were a repentant sinner, is offered a chance
to leave his penitence behind and change the world. After
all, as Luke tells us, he was "hungry" (4:2). So why not do
something? Why not organize the engines of compassion
and feed the world? Why not mobilize the resources of the
church to lead the world in what appears, by all accounts,
to be a noble and quite necessary effort? Why not *be* the
world's Savior and play a useful role?

Yet, surprisingly, Jesus refuses. In fact, his refusal
sets a pattern for refusals that punctuate his whole ministry,
refusals to play the role the Pharisees assign to him, to play
the role the disciples assign to him, to play the role, in the
end, Jerusalem and Rome assign to him. So he refuses: "It
is written, 'You shall not live by bread alone.'" Useless. He
could set the world free from hunger. He could forever be
thought of as the world's benefactor and thereby assure a
hearing for religion as the nourishing freedom of civilized
people. But he refuses. Religion does not evidently set one
free, any more than a full belly does. How strange those
words sound to us, who have grown to appreciate both the
usefulness of religion and the fullness of our bellies. God
sets free, he implies, and God's freedom sets people free,
not to sate their hunger but to discover their hunger for
him.[1]

Clearly, this freedom does not relieve the church of
feeding the hungry, but it does suggest another basis for it
than mere compassion or the useful function it provides society. Compassion wears out and society finds it not too

difficult to forget. The church engages in the task of feeding the hungry because the church confesses as a matter of faith that eating is sacramental, i.e., the hunger for food is, at its heart, the hunger for God. That is why the marriage feast of the lamb is such a climactic symbol for the coming kingdom; at that banquet table all are fed. It is precisely this connection between daily bread and the bread of life that the devil seeks to sever in reducing the gospel to a merely material reality and which the church is often so willing to forget in reducing the whole matter to merely a spiritual reality. In both instances the assumption seems to be that faith, to mean anything, has to prove itself useful to the world. And it is precisely that view of his own ministry and the ministry of the church that Jesus rejects in his assertion of freedom from the world's definition of Savior. He is willing, at that point, to be useless to the world, even to say "No" to it. The freedom of the world has, rather, to do with being made free for God, an act in which we do indeed eat and drink our own salvation but do so only by means of a broken body and poured out blood. Only there do we taste and see the goodness of the Lord; only there do we show forth the Lord's death to all schemes of human salvation; only there are we set free to discern our redemptive hunger.

The uselessness of Jesus Christ in the face of human starvation announces, in this first act of the story, Jesus' strange notion of his own freedom. The devil shows him up to be a useless Savior. And Jesus accepts that designation, arguing that salvation is not a measure of his being judged useful to humanity but, rather, of being obedient to God. In such uselessness "humanity" is redefined. No longer can it be seen as that vague collection of individuals whose possession of natural rights is somehow self-evident, and self-evidently significant. Instead, humanity is that person created for life with God, that person who lives and, in fact, discovers his own freedom, not in the number of increasing options laid out before him, but in the attention to the one thing needful. Accordingly, salvation begins to emerge as the most useless thing in the world, i.e., being united with this man who refused to serve "humanity," i.e., who refused to feed the hungry, and who, instead, fed on every word that proceeded from the mouth of God. In embryo in this first act is the entire gospel. Jesus' work of redemption can be read from beginning to end as the overcoming of salvation, the end, if you will, of strategies of repentance, of politics, of therapy, of technique. In this sense the cross is the end of salvation. That, after all, is the whole point of those who taunt Jesus: "He saved others; he cannot save himself." (Matt.27:42) This is true. He is a lousy Savior. What kind of Savior is it that cannot save himself? Would any sensible yuppie bent on success, not only in the business world but also in the company of other successful Christians, have anything to do with this loser? The cross is the end of salvation. There is no point in lusting after it anymore. All that the cross leaves us with is a dead Jesus, as useless a thing to the world as a stone which refuses to become bread, as a benefactor who refuses to play the role.

If Jesus will not play the economic role, then, perhaps he will play the political role. The devil holds a summit conference with this difficult rabbi, in which he offers him not only all the authority and glory the world has to give but, even more, the opportunity for Jesus to remake that world after his own image. We know that Jesus rejects this offer too, and we are perhaps not that surprised since the cost of such power would be for him to crook the knee to the devil himself, an act of apostasy as obvious as it would be unlikely. Yet, though Scripture is often clear, it is never obvious, and least of all here. The temptation has to do with worship; Jesus clearly says as much in quoting Scripture: "It is written, 'You shall worship the Lord your God, and him only shall you serve.'"(Luke 4: 8) But what's the big deal about worship? I mean, who cares, finally?

Let me offer an example as to why Jesus' reply is so unobviously disturbing at this point. It has to do, as does this passage, with the question as to the "real world." Whose world is it, after all? Is it the world of the Lord our God, whom to worship is the highest and most fulfilling of human callings, and in whose world all other callings testify in ways large and small to the fact that we are his? Or is it someone else's world, perhaps no one's, in which "the kingdoms of this world" must get along the best they can, adopting various strategies of salvation or therapies for coping. If it is the former, worship will always appear strangely useless, even though it is that world's (secret) strength; if it is the latter, worship will always be immensely useful, even though, in the end, it will trivialize the faith and evacuate it of power.

It was my son's first year of high school, and my wife and I were invited to meet his teachers on "Parents' Night." We went to all his classes and took special interest in his English teacher and his math and history and science teachers. We listened to their presentations of method and subject-matter, and, at the end of the evening, we felt more or less satisfied. There were some strong points and weak points, but, then, no school is perfect. There was only one class left to go to, and it was not a "solid," i.e., a full-credit class; it was called "health," and I supposed it dealt with matters of hygiene and, perhaps, exercise. Reluctantly, my wife and I went, thinking we would just complete the schedule. The teacher began with her presentation, in which, in short order, she touched on the topics of AIDS, teen-age pregnancy, homelessness, abuse of children, and even the tensions between races, all of which were not only timely but issues confronting every child in that school. All of a sudden "health" had taken on a whole new meaning for me, and I became convinced that this was one of the most important classes my son would be taking that fall. After her presentation, I went up to the teacher and asked what resources she used in dealing with such issues; did she, for instance, attempt to lift up for consideration any biblical insights or permit any of the students to articulate their faith? She took me, I am sure, for a meddling fundamentalist, but, in any case, with a withering glare she informed me that this was a public school and not a school of Christian indoctrination.

To be sure, I agreed, nor would it be an advance, I think, to have public institutions enforce matters of faith. But I wondered that night, and still do, how it is that young

people, or, indeed, anyone, can deal with the problems of
AIDS, for example, not to mention race, without having
their deepest convictions challenged, and without being
able to examine and re-examine their faith. From the
school's standpoint, faith was useless in this discussion. Its
insights had been ruled out *ab initio* and were therefore not
taken seriously. In a not so subtle way, faith as the ground
for ethical behavior is found similarly useless by many
large state universities. They do not teach it; it cannot be
that important. And, as a result, racial problems are never
viewed as a matter of faith, as, in fact, a *theological* issue at
its very heart, but rather as a matter of human ignorance, a
problem best solved by more courses in "health." So we
combat AIDS by handing out condoms, and we deal with
the virulence of racism by offering courses in sensitivity
training, thereby witnessing to our profound faith in both
technology and therapy as the most useful means of human
salvation. The third member of this unholy trinity is, admit-
tedly, religion, in which we also have profound faith and
which we find quite useful, and often the public debate is
about how to parcel out time and resources among these
three saviors. The point of this example, however, is not
how to get religion taught in the public schools (which is
just another effort to make the faith useful and, therefore, a
trivialization of faith) but rather to suggest that the question
"Whom do you worship?" underlies nearly every public issue we face. And, indeed, it is when that question begins to
surface that our gods and our goals begin to emerge.

In any case, Jesus, when engaged in a political discussion with the devil, cuts straight to the bone: the exercise of political power is rooted in faith; the most profound
political question concerns whom one worships. "It is written 'You shall worship the Lord your God, and him only
shall you serve.'" (Matt 4:8) That is *the* political issue:
whom do we worship? And it is the answer one gives to
that that makes the answers to all the other issues so difficult. Not easier, but more difficult. Which is why religion is
so useful and faith so useless. Religion always wants to
make things easier; it "solves" the AIDS issue or problems

of race by means of morality or therapy or even technology, thereby proving its usefulness to the culture. Faith, on the other hand, makes things more difficult by refusing to see these "problems" as problems, i.e., as amenable to solution by a culture and a church pervaded by sin. All faith can do *is* worship. All faith can do *is* to confess. To be sure, confessing faith in the cross of Jesus Christ is hardly an answer, and yet such a confession defines how those without answers shall go about seeking them. Worship is not oriented toward "problem-solving" but rather toward faithful living in the midst of "problems" that are not so much "solved" as they are named. After all, those who declared their faith at Barmen were not seeking to provide Nazi Germany with better answers to its economic, political, or even racial problems, but they were seeking to provide Nazi Germany with a better *faith* than that which Naziism was calling for. In that sense, the church sought, in confessing its faith in God, to name what was not God. And in the event, the Nazis understood what the church was saying right well. Indeed, how much better would the Nazis have preferred a church that contented itself with the promotion of various social or political strategies. Such might have, indeed, been useful; strategies can be endlessly debated. It is the confession of faith, the question, "Whom do we worship?" which is truly threatening. Or again, Martin Luther King, Jr., did not hesitate (anymore than Abraham Lincoln before him) to use biblical language in the most public of forums to make his political points. When he was in the Birmingham jail, the question he raised to the White ministers who objected to his activities, was not how best to solve Birmingham's economic or even racial problems, but whom, in fact, to worship, and what kind of faith God was compelling the church in the South to confess.[2] Here, as in Luke's gospel, the most obvious political question—Who governs?—becomes at its heart, the most unobvious theological question—Whom do we worship?

All of which is to set the stage for what is clearly the climactic episode in Luke's portrayal of Jesus' temptation to become useful, and that concerns the matter of religion itself. In this scene Jesus is taken to the pinnacle of the temple, and the devil invites him, in effect, to take the leap of faith, to prove that he is God's favorite by compelling God to save him from destruction. In a strange way this invitation is a perversion of the journey Abraham and Isaac took up Mt. Moriah. There Abraham was also tested and invited to make the terrible choice between the child of promise (in whom the promise of Abraham's own salvation resided) or the Lord who had promised. Even in that unhinging scene, however, it is already clear that the choice is between choosing salvation and choosing God; between, if you will, religion and faith. And when, in the end, Abraham gives up salvation in order to follow this Lord, he can only receive his son (and his own salvation), as if this Lord had raised Isaac from the dead, that is, as if Isaac and the salvific promise he represents were Abraham's now solely by grace.

So it is that the question religion poses is whether one worships salvation or whether one lives by grace. It is important to keep this question in mind because it is precisely the one that arises in this scene. Can Jesus be made religiously useful? That is the tempting question the devil poses. The threat in this story, the real threat to faith, is not, then, the devil in the guise of war or pestilence or death but, rather, in the guise of the religious seeker after truth. He quotes Scripture as if he were the soul of piety itself:[3] "He will give his angels charge of you, to guard you," and "On their hands they will bear you up, lest you dash your foot against a stone." (Matt 4:10) In what precisely, though, does the temptation consist? How is it that Jesus could become religiously useful?

The temptation consists in the invitation to Jesus to become a martyr. As T.S. Eliot has noted, this temptation is always the "greatest treason."[4] And, in fact, it is a temptation, in part, because it so closely resembles the truth. In the end, Jesus did give up his life; in the end, he did not save it; in the end, he was made captive, taunted, killed for the sake of his faith. He did not have to go this way; he could have chosen to go another. Yet he was faithful and pursued the will of his Father even to death on the cross.

And so, the only issue here is why wait. If following obediently, even to the point of losing one's life, constitutes, in fact, true faith, why not make it a strategy for winning divine approval? Indeed, what the devil gives Jesus is the opportunity at the very outset of his ministry to find in self-sacrifice the supreme form of self-glorification, always the most religious of temptations.[5] And, indeed, why wait? If martyrdom is the way to freedom, why not sooner rather than later? Waiting is, in fact . . . useless. Which is why we should not be surprised that Jesus refuses also this temptation and instead . . . waits. "And Jesus answered him. It is said, 'You shall not tempt the Lord your God.'" (Matt 4:12) "And when the devil had ended every temptation, he departed from him until an opportune time." (Matt 4:13)

Jesus waits because waiting is an act of faith in which attention is given to the will of God, even above one's quest for salvation. Indeed, in this last temptation of Christ, it is the lust for salvation that is portrayed as the enemy of faith, a lust that seeks its own glory and its own power wholly apart from the will of God. And no more than a hungry Jesus is seduced by the usefulness of bread or a weakened Jesus by the usefulness of power, so here a waiting Jesus is content to wait, to attend to God even at the risk of appearing useless to a world eager to save itself.

So it is that "waiting" becomes the form of Jesus' faith, a form which should be instructive to a church that is frightened of waiting. So frightened are we of such waiting that when we hear talk of it, we can only think that what is meant by it is yet another strategy. Accordingly, there is no more tempting stratagem of faith than the adoption of no strategy, as if waiting might itself become a good strategy for the church's success. Then, instead of jumping off the pinnacle of the temple, we would just wait there hoping that our waiting would produce the same effect as jumping, i.e., that our self-sacrifice would pay off. But Jesus waits not as a strategy but out of obedience. But can not obedience prove to be the ultimate strategy? To be sure, that is always a possibility, just as martyrdom can provide the most delicious of satisfactions. Faithful waiting, on the other hand, waits on God's freedom to judge and to call; faithful waiting is willing to be in the wrong over against God, willing, in fact, to wait only in the company of those who have been judged wrong over against God, i.e., only in the company of the quite sinful church. That is also why Jesus Christ waits in this temptation story: he will not be saved apart from that community of sinners, the church. *Extra ecclesiam nulla salus!* Outside that community, there is no salvation, because apart from those conniving and scheming sinners, Jesus Christ refuses to live a more "spiritual", i.e., a more useful life.

So the useless Savior begins his ministry, and, even at the outset, we can begin to see the outline of the story. For what is his waiting but finally a passion; what is his refusal of salvation but finally a rejection that will lead to his being rejected on the cross; what is his uselessness but finally an unwillingness to save himself? All of that is prefigured in this temptation story, a story of obedience in faith and, yet, a story in which the uselessness of the Savior begins to describe a deeper kind of freedom, a freedom for God which has no interest in the strategies of salvation. Precisely such strategies are rejected again and again as being at odds with faith. Indeed, such strategies are seen as threatening, in part because they would separate Jesus from the hungry, from the powerless, from the sinful. Time and time again he refuses to become a virtuoso of religion, a hero of the faith, a benefactor of human compassion and industry. Instead, he takes his place in solidarity with sinful Israel ("It is written . . . "!) and, therefore, with all of us, and refuses to think that that is an unsuitable thing for a Messiah to do. In fact, he does the most useless thing of all and becomes one of us, even to the point of loving us so much that he simply refuses any salvation at all that does not include the useless, i.e., those who cannot save themselves, i.e., everyone. Here, as elsewhere, the devil's real work is to separate us from the love of Christ, and he attempts to do so in no more subtle way than by rendering faith useful. Jesus, in believing for us, refuses to bite, and in so doing looks utterly useless. As useless, indeed, as an empty tomb.

NOTES

1. Simone Weil, *Waiting for God*, (New York: Perennial Library, 1973). "The danger is not lest the soul should doubt whether there is any bread [God], but lest, by a lie, it should persuade itself that it is not hungry. It can only persuade itself of this by lying, for the reality of its hunger is not a belief, it is a certainty." p. 35.

2. Taylor Branch, *Parting the Waters*, (Edinburgh: Simon and Schuster, 1988). King wrote: "I have heard numerous religious leaders of the South call upon worshipers to comply with a desegregation decision because it is the *law*, . . .but I have longed to hear white ministers say 'follow this decree16 because integration is morally *right* and the Negro is your brother. . . .' I have wept over the laxity of the church. But be assured that my tears have been tears of love. . . ." , pp. 743-743

3. Karl Barth, *Church Dogmatics*, IV/1, ed. G. W. Bromiley and T. F. Torrance, (Edinburgh: T. & T. Clark, 1961), p. 262.

4. T. S. Eliot, *Murder in the Cathedral*, (London: Faber and Faber, 1937), part I, p. 44.

5. Karl Barth, *Ibid.*, p. 263.

2

The Uselessness of God:
The Doctrine of The Trinity in the Life of The Church

The ironsmith fashions it and works it over the coals; he shapes it with hammers, and forges it with his strong arm; he becomes hungry and his strength fails, he drinks no water and is faint. The carpenter stretches a line, he marks it out with a pencil; he fashions it with planes, and marks it with a compass; he shapes it into the figure of a man, with the beauty of a man, to dwell in a house. He cuts down cedars; or he chooses a holm tree or an oak and lets it grow strong among the trees of the forest; he plants a cedar and the rain nourishes it. Then it becomes fuel for a man; he takes a part of it and warms himself; also he makes a god and worships it, he makes it a graven image and falls down before it. Half of it he burns in the fire; over the half he eats flesh, he roasts meat and is satisfied; also he warms himself and says "Aha, I am warm, I have seen the fire!" And the rest of it he makes into a god, his idol; and falls down to it and worships it; he prays to it and says, "Deliver me, for thou art my god!"

They know not, nor do they discern; for he has shut their eyes so that they cannot see, and their minds, so that they cannot understand. No one considers, nor is there knowledge or discernment to say "Half of it I burned in the fire, I also baked bread on its coals, I roasted flesh and have eaten; and shall I make the residue of it an abomination? Shall I fall down before a block of wood?

Isaiah 44: 12-19

There is no place where the usefulness of God is
more deeply affirmed than in our own country. Indeed, it
sounds almost unpatriotic to speak of the uselessness of
God, and, in a way, it is. The baptismal certificate of our
nation's founding, the Declaration of Independence, testi-
fies in every place to the usefulness of God as "Creator," as
"Nature's God," and even as "divine Providence." Lest one
grow uneasy about this "God-language," Jefferson makes it
clear that the Creator's truths are, in any case, "self-
evident," and, hence, a close reading of "Nature" itself. One
should not belittle, however, either Jefferson's language or
his theology, for it is quite clear that he thinks the very definition of what it is to be human (i.e., to be "endowed with
certain unalienable rights," etc.) is determined by relation
to this Creator. Indeed, it is creation itself that constitutes
our primary relation to God, so much so that Jefferson is
quite content to let the title "Creator" encompass the entirety of God's being and work. However, in the absence of any
other information about God, the title "Creator" leaves
open the question as to what creation is for. One might jus-
tifiably conclude that it is for "life, liberty and the pursuit
of happiness," the creation, in short, of the "heavenly city
of the 18th Century philosophers."[1] But even were this to be
true, it is difficult to see how one can refrain from concluding that, at least in our founding document, God exists in
order to assure our happiness, a rather startling reversal of
Westminster's definition of our chief end.

A god whose chief end is to create human beings so
that they may enjoy themselves forever is a useful god indeed. Moreover, if our primary relation to this Creator is
through creation itself, then what becomes increasingly ali-
en to our humanity, not to say useless, is the story of Jesus
Christ. For example, if what it means to be a human being
can be self-evidently read off from nature, then, at best,
Jesus' humanity must be worked into that picture and, at
worst, excised altogether as something strange and incom-
prehensible. (Jefferson himself leaves us a witness to his
bafflement at the figure of Jesus in his own edition of the
New Testament.[2] What kind of God, after all, would choose

to reveal himself in a definition of human life that, in effect, gave up "life, liberty and the pursuit of happiness" and who, having done so, would call such foolishness "gospel"?)

There is not much room in the "heavenly city" for the cross. Whatever else might be said about it, that is not what this "Creator" had in mind in endowing his creatures with "unalienable rights." Unalienable rights belong to those whose pursuit of happiness is indistinguishable from self-fulfillment, from self-enhancement. The baptism of every American into the birthright of happiness is the founding act, then, in building a culture of narcissists. Indeed, there is a direct line between the Declaration's notion of a god whose work is exhausted in creation and the nihilism of our culture's obsession with self-creation, self-realization. Making God useful means making God useful to what is self-evidently important to me, an assumption which, in Jefferson's deistic philosophy, might prove benign enough, but in the hands of less "happy" philosophes might well lead to such "self-evident truths" that blacks, for example, are sub-human, or that Jews are vermin, or even that abortion is simply a private matter.

The truth of the matter is that the idea of God can be made to serve any number of abhorrent causes and none so easily or so well as the ones we value, i.e., the "good" uses. The question, though, is not how we then purify our idea of God so that we ascend to a more rarefied definition but, rather, how we attend to what is not at all self-evident, to what appears to be a scandalously conceived, if not totally useless, self-giving on God's part, a self-giving and self-naming, however, in which God does not exist simply as a function of our giving and naming, in which, in other words, God is free.

But how to speak of such a God? Why not use the term, "Creator"? It is interesting to note that in our very different day God is being named once again as "Creator," especially as a substitute for "Father."[3] The rationale for this undertaking stems from the conviction among some that "Father" imports sexist language into our notion of God and that "Creator," being gender-neutral, is, therefore, a purification of such language. "If God is male," writes Mary Daly, "the male is God."[4] Such an argument would indeed carry substantial weight if what was meant by the term "Father" was that God was to be construed primarily (i.e., *named*) as *my* Father, perhaps on some analogy to my earthly Father. If this were true, then there might well be a good reason to substitute the word "Creator" as the name for God, rather than "Father." After all, if the *primary* relation between God and the world is (self-evident? experientially?) established through me and my perceptions, affirmations, and even sexuality, then those very important parts of my identity will determine what kind of God I am able to worship and know. Indeed, there is nothing in any part of my identity that would allow me to argue, in principle, that it represents a more authentic way of speaking of God than some other person's way. If, then, it is true that the male is God because the God whom we worship has been construed as male, then it is at least as true that the female has a right to be God because she can construe God only according to her identity.

Interestingly, the one theological conviction the feminist critique of trinitarian language has in common with Jefferson's more optimistic deism is a deep reluctance to speak of Jesus Christ as the *revelation* of God with us. For Jefferson, "self-evident truths" meant that, among other things, Jesus Christ was not needed; he was, in fact, an embarrassment to the exercise of human rights and the fulfillment of human life. To be human meant that whatever one might say of God was as open to being true or false as what someone else might say on the basis of experience or reason. There were no "privileged" points of view, or, rather, all points of view were equally privileged but, were so not by virtue of a special grace grasped in faith, but rather, by virtue of the canon of reason apprehending nature and nature's God. The one point of view excluded, however, was that which would question the basis for privilege in the "self-evident" laws of nature, arguing, in effect, that such a basis might itself be deeply vitiated, if not broken altogether. The problem is not whether "faith" is more privileged than "reason" but whether either one is privileged to speak of God at all. Similarly, the same question arises on feminist grounds as to whether substituting "Creator" for "Father" puts us any closer to understanding *God*. The question, again, is not whether the "masculine" (whatever that means) view is more privileged than a "feminine" one (whatever that means) but whether either one is inherently privileged at all.

Now this questioning of the virtues of self-evidence (and of the experience of being male or female)[5] sounds, especially in Jefferson's America, pessimistic. If all views of God are deeply vitiated such that human discourse about him is fatally flawed and human self-knowledge chimerical, then how can this seem anything but bad news? If nothing else, the questioning of self-evidence or the questioning of the revelatory capacity of experience, sounds faintly oppressive, as if faith meant the denial of life, liberty, and the pursuit of happiness, indeed, as if faith meant not an enhancing or deepening of life but its emptying.

I do not think this charge against the faith, namely, that it is pessimistic, should be dismissed out of hand. The Roman Empire, after all, accused the early church of being "haters of the human race." The gospel is scandalous. The birth of the king does threaten, and threatens most of all our petty kingdoms defining life, liberty, and the pursuit of happiness. In fact, the questioning of self-evidence as the ground for speaking about God as a general possibility does more than raise charges of pessimism from a culture of self-realization; it subverts that culture. Feminist critiques of sexist God-language are, strangely, not subversive of the culture. Their complaint about a sexist culture has nothing to do with that culture's self-realizing tendencies but only with finding a place among them. Similarly, liberationist theologians are quite able to co-exist with self-evident calls to happiness if they can contribute their own definitions. What subverts the culture of self-realization most radically is that definition of life, liberty, and the pursuit of happiness that is described in the cross. From the point of view of self-realization, such a cross is useless; from the point of view of faith, such a cross is life.

Which is why the doctrine of the Trinity, derided by many both inside and outside the church as insignificant, is, in fact, the most subversive confessional statement about God that the church has to make to the culture. For the doctrine of the Trinity claims that God cannot be reduced simply to a function of what he does or can do for us, that, in fact, God is free from us. This does not mean that God is free from us because "self-evidently" he is a trinitarian mystery beyond our knowing. The doctrine of the Trinity knows of a freedom of God because it knows that the God who is free from us is free for us in Jesus Christ, the very one in whom he names himself as Father, Son, and Holy Spirit. There, in Jesus Christ, i.e., not "self-evidently," not in my heart, not in my experience as a man or as a woman, but there, in Jesus Christ, God himself gives himself to be known.[6] And that means that to know Jesus Christ, to confess him Lord is immediately to be baptized into his crucified and raised humanity and, by *grace*, to be given a share in his knowledge of the Father in the Son by the Holy Spirit. The God who meets us in Jesus Christ is the God who identifies himself as the Crucified; the god who meets us elsewhere is much more malleable and, in the end, quite willing to be a function of our own naming. Only the crucified God names himself as triune.

And only the triune God names himself as the God of the church. Alvin Kimel has written that "if the triune name . . . identifies the Christian Church, this is because the appellation first and primarily identifies the God of the church."[7] Those who find the doctrine of the Trinity a hindrance in speaking of God will, in the end, not only resent the centrality of Jesus Christ for faith, but also find the church a burdensome appendage.[8] For it is the church that is baptized in the name of the Father, Son, and Holy Spirit, and, hence, it is the church which, in Jesus Christ, is called to worship this God and live as his community.

And it is the church that learns from this name not a denying of human life but its definition; not the eliminating of human freedom but its incarnation; not the scorning of human happiness but its true beatitude. After all, why is it that the church insisted on speaking of God in trinitarian terms in the first place? Was it not because the church's profound conviction that "*God* was in Christ reconciling the world to himself" was being challenged? Was it not Arius who, in effect, denied that God was in Christ? Is this not the threat that constantly challenges the church's confessing, a threat that holds that God does not really meet us in Jesus Christ, but only a good example; that God does not really set us free by dying, but only by giving us useful information, information that restores our self-esteem and helps us realize ourselves? Is this not the beginning of the broad road to "self-evidence" and the nihilistic emptiness of the frantic pursuit of happiness?

Geoffrey Wainwright has noted how shallow and vague Jefferson's "self-evident truths" can be and how, in contrast, the very words "life, liberty, and the pursuit of happiness" are "charged with meaning from the biblical story of creation, redemption, and final salvation under the guidance of the triune God." He goes on to ask, "How are Christians to maintain and command their distinctive belief and teaching concerning a God who did not by an initial origination of the world then become otiose, but rather so loved a fallen world as to give his only Son for its redemption and send the Holy Spirit for its transformation?"[9] Or, to put it another way, Martha Stortz writes: "It would be easy for a 'Creator' to sacrifice a 'Christ.' Perhaps the category 'sacrifice' would not even apply. It is not so easy for a Father to sacrifice a Son. Yet this is the story of our faith. We could choose another story—Creator, Christ, and Spirit; the Mother, the Son, and the Bulrushes—but then we would have to choose another faith and another confession of faith."[10] Only the story of Jesus Christ compels us to take the triune God seriously, and only there do we find the critical center of our faith. For only there is the forgiveness of sin a matter of God's own being, his freedom to be God in this way and not another. Only there, in the obedience of the Son, do we learn to pray, "Our Father. . . ."

The church stands or falls as it is able to confess that God is Father, Son, and Holy Spirit. Such a confession is not at all self-evident, much less is it the fruit of wisdom or experience or self-awareness. It is, rather, the fruit of Jesus Christ,[11] the scandalous content of his history and life. For in him we do not just "see" this triune mystery, as if his business were to disclose some puzzle to us, but in him we meet the God who, in loving us, loves us for his purposes, forgives us out of his own eternal decision, unites us in his own life. The freedom of the triune God is not an invitation to increase our options in the pursuit of our ever more individually construed happiness but, rather, the invitation to be free for God, finding in his self-relatedness the freedom to be genuinely *for* one another and to live in community. It is only in the freedom of this God that freedom itself can be re-conceived, thought of now not as something to be snatched, but emptying itself, taking the form of a servant, becoming obedient unto death, even death on the cross. And, indeed, it is only in the freedom of this God that freedom itself can, in fact, become truly exalted, receiving *a name which is above every name,* that at the name of Jesus, *every* knee should bow . . . to the glory of God the Father.

In effect, it is the doctrine of the Trinity that witnesses to the distinctiveness of God, that reminds the church not only of God's freedom but also of our own. To be free for this God is to resist the temptation to idolatry. The triune God names himself; all other gods we can name. The doctrine of the Trinity, then, is the first line of defense against the work of "that factory of idols"[12] we know so well.

Surely that is the significance of Isaiah's satirical description of the technology of idolatry in the 44th chapter. How can something we create escape our flawed mortality and become greater than its creator? We find a tree; we use part of it to warm ourselves, part of it to cook our supper, and part of it we worship. On the whole, we find the tree very useful, and we find it just as useful for religious purposes as we do for culinary. We use the tree to pursue our happiness.

Idols are useful. That is why we create them. Israel's problem was not a surrounding culture of atheism that denied God's existence but, rather, a culture suffused with religion. Gods were everywhere. The issue before Israel was not how to get people to start talking about religion but, in fact, how to hear God's voice amidst the competing uproar of religious noise. The question was, "Which God ought I *obey*?" "To whom do I owe allegiance?" "Thou shalt have no other gods before me" suggests that, in fact, the chief theological problem Israel faced was idolatry. Are we so different? Is our problem that we cannot find God? Or is it, rather, that the God whom we cannot escape does not seem useful enough to us? Isaiah sees the uselessness of God, but he knows that, in finding us, this God, unlike all others, reveals to us uses not at all self-evident and, in the event, quite surprising. God, Isaiah says, surprises. And God surprises us most of all in his refusal to be used, a refusal not seen in his sheer mystery but, rather, in his revealed presence, in his decision to be for us *as God,* and to be God *for us*, as Father, Son, and Holy Spirit. Nothing less.

It is in following this God that Israel learns not only to laugh at an intimidating culture's preoccupation with its useful little deities, but also to challenge the very roots of that culture's captivity by offering her own praise and service to God. Israel does not learn of injustice and the poverty of widows and orphans from the useful gods organizing the culture's self-realization. Rather, it is the free God whose ways are *not* our ways, whose thoughts are *not* our thoughts, who reveals to Israel what justice means in the context of his loving purpose. In similar fashion, the disciples are not drawn from useless lives of idleness or boredom to follow Jesus Christ but from quite acceptable occupations in fishing, tax-collecting, tent-making. They learn from him, sometimes in quite startling language (e.g., "Look at the birds of the air . . . . Consider the lilies of the field" Matt: 6:26, 28) of a life that can only appear from the culture's point of view to be useless but from the standpoint of the faith, the only real definition of life. And how hard it is to learn. Time and again Jesus refuses to accede to their

demands to render his teaching more useful. But in his
company and before a cross none of them thought necessary, these so useful disciples became in fact, salt, leaven,
light, fishers of men. And they became so not because they
had discovered a strategy that "worked," much less because
they finally "found" themselves, but because the *freedom* of
God had rendered their agenda useless and, in doing so,
made them, for the first time, useful. Philemon can only become useful when he receives his slave Onesimus ("Useful"), no longer as his slave, but as his brother (rendering
him useless as a slave), joining him in slavery to Christ.

So what? That is, among other things, a theological
question. One might ask what difference any of this makes
to anybody. Who cares, after all, if we honor the freedom
of God by confessing him as Father, Son, and Holy Spirit
(and thereby confess ourselves to be sisters and brothers in
Christ and, in him, the church of this God), or whether we
give this God a convenient label and get on with things?

An answer to such a question might begin with a
look at the pivotal theological controversy of this century, a
controversy that resulted in the church confessing its faith
in "The Barmen Declaration." In fact, here, too, atheism
was not the problem. No, here the problem arose in connection with the Nazi effort to render the church useful to the
Third Reich. The issue before the church was both painful-
ly and, one must also say, happily, clear. Should it become
useful to the culture? Does God meet us truly and fully and
finally in Jesus Christ, or does he, alongside this Jesus
Christ, (and therefore not exclusively in him, and perhaps
also not *really* in him) meet us in the form of another, an
Adolf Hitler, perhaps, or in the "blood and soil" of Germany itself or even in the genes of the Aryan race? A great
deal depended on the answer the church gave to such a
question. In any case, the invitation, when it came to the
church, was an invitation to become . . . useful.

The church responded to this invitation not by offering an analysis of Nazi culture nor by developing a strategy
that would allow the church to maneuver within some larg-
er, perhaps National Socialist, perhaps not, context. Instead,

weak as it was and incomprehensive as it may appear today, the Barmen Declaration *confessed* the church's faith in
God, in the free God who *alone* meets us in Jesus Christ,
who *alone* is the Lord of the church, and who *alone* is to be
honored above all. The *political* relevance of the first com-
mandment was seen to be explosively clear. It is the *freedom* of God that this world finds most threatening, for it is
the freedom of God that alone *resists* the world's efforts to
realize itself. The children of darkness are not really bothered by the ideologies of the children of light; the latter
might even prove useful. What threatens the children of
darkness is the *faith* of the children of light, faith in the
God who is free, who, in triumphing *over* us in Jesus
Christ, sets us free to call him "Father," to live as his free
children in his Son, to live and even to die for one another
in his Spirit.

The Barmen Declaration is Christ-centered, trinitarian in faith, and evangelical in spirit. It is clearly the work
of the church. Because it does not try to be useful politically (i.e., as a strategy), it is the most politically relevant document the church has produced in this century. Because it
confesses its faith in the free God, it speaks powerfully to
the ideologies which always threaten what belongs to God.
Because it refuses to use God, it has proven to be the most
useful confessional statement in the church today. Listen to
its concluding article:

> Lo, I am with you always to the close of the age. (Matt.
> 28:20) The Word of God is not fettered. (2 Timothy 2:9)
>
> The church's commission, on which its *freedom* [my
> italics] is founded, consists in delivering the message of
> the free grace of God to all people in Christ's stead, and
> therefore in the ministry of his own Word and work
> through sermon and sacrament.
>
> We reject the false doctrine, as though the Church in
> human arrogance could place the Word and work of the
> Lord in the service of any arbitrarily chosen desires, pur-
> poses, and plans.[13]

So what? To be sure, God's freedom will survive our foolishness. Even the church will survive insofar as God has promised never to be without witness. And it is true that we live by his promise, not by our theological determinations. Yet, if it is the free God we are called to serve, then we betray that calling and confess the hopelessness of our own captivity if we content ourselves merely with being useful to the culture. God has not called us to be busy or important or even humble—only faithful. He loves the world, the world that is so busy and so important and even so humble that it misses the one gift the Father gives in the Son through the Spirit: it misses Jesus Christ. It would be a shame if we left to join Martha in her "humble" serving, joined in the excuses of such busy folk who could not come to the banquet, joined the elder brother whose self-importance could only sulk while the Father sacrificed a fatted calf for a useless son. No, the New Testament does not really offer dire threats or intimidating curses on those who fail to celebrate with Jesus Christ; rather, the gospels leave such folk to gnaw on the roots of their own bitterness. They miss the kingdom, as if it were nothing more than a bus. Such folk, Jesus reminds us, have their own reward. Hell, C.S. Lewis once remarked, has no locked gates; one can walk out any time. Which is why the gospel is always about freedom, and yet so baffling to those who would prefer their own darkness. Still, it is that freedom that the world cannot give itself, the glorious, unexpected, unwarranted, unmanipulatable freedom of the children of God, the children adopted into the Son of the Father by the Holy Spirit. It is enough to make one laugh, which, one supposes, is what the divine comedy is all about.

NOTES

1. Carl Becker, *The Heavenly City of the Eighteenth Century Philosophers.* (New Haven: Yale University Press, 1932). Becker interprets Jefferson in light of his acceptance of Locke's ideas. For an alter-

native view, cf. Gary Wills' *Inventing America, Jefferson's Declaration of Independence,* (New York: Doubleday, 1978). Wills thinks Jefferson is much more in debt to the school of Scottish Common Sense Philosophy. In this school "self-evidence" far from being a kind of perfect abstraction, incapable of grounding other propositions (as in Locke's epistemology), is, instead, a truth which the mind can firmly grasp, and grasp, not by argumentation or reasoning, but by its constitution as a created, rational mind. A self-evident truth, then, is a truth that the mind cannot help but grasp directly in its very nature as mind. Jefferson hoped then to "place before mankind the common sense of the subject in terms so plain and firm as to command their assent." p. 191.

2. Jefferson wrote, "Do we want to know what God is? Search not the book called Scripture, which any human hand might make, but the scripture called creation." Cited in "The Faith of the Founding Fathers," David Gill, in *One Nation Under God,* (Waco, Texas: Word Books, 1975), p. 41. Gill continues: "Jefferson spent a part of his life editing out forty-six pages of 'acceptable' parts of Jesus' teaching from the Gospels. What was left he called the most sublime and benevolent code of morals which has ever been offered to man."(p.42) Sidney Ahlstrom in his *A Religious History of the American People,* (New Haven: Yale University Press, 1972), p. 367, joins Saul Padover in calling Jefferson the "St. Paul of American democracy," an ironic encomium in that Jefferson abominated the apostle who, he thought, had corrupted the pure teachings of Jesus. In spite of Gary Wills' efforts to interpret Jefferson as a scientist, as opposed to a theologian (op.cit. p.365), I find it hard to disagree with G.K. Chesterton that the Declaration of Independence is preeminently a theological document. "America is the only nation in the world that is founded on a creed. The creed is set forth with dogmatic and even theological lucidity in the Declaration. . . ." (cited in Wills, *op.cit.,* p. xxi).

3. Donald Bloesch, *The Battle For the Trinity,* (Ann Arbor, Michigan: Vine Books, 1985), pp. 43-55.

4. Mary Daly, *Beyond God the Father,* (Boston: Beacon Press, 1973), p. 19.

5. Donald Bloesch, *op.cit.* "For nearly all feminists, the final court of appeal is human experience, particularly feminine experience." p. 57

6. Wilhelm Niesel, *Reformed Symbolics.* trans. David Lewis, (Edinburgh: Oliver and Boyd, 1962). "The doctrine of the Trinity is not

there to undergird a mysticism of being with a Christian coloring. On the contrary it is intended to bear witness to the fact that in Jesus Christ it is God Himself who comes to meet us." p. 141. Cf. also, Thomas F. Torrance, "Karl Barth and the Latin Heresy" in *Scottish Journal of Theology*, vol. 39, no. 4, (1986): pp. 461-482.

7. Alvin Kimel, "The God Who Likes His Name," in *Interpretation*, (April, 1991): p. 149.

8. Geoffrey Wainwright, "The Doctrine of the Trinity" in *Interpretation*, (April 1991): p. 123.

9. *Ibid.*, p. 124.

10. Donald Bloesch, *op.cit.*, p. 52.

11. Karl Barth, *Church Dogmatics*, I/1, ed. G. W. Bromiley and T. F. Torrance, (Edinburgh: T. & T. Clark, 1963), "The Root of the Doctrine of the Trinity," pp. 349-383.

12. John Calvin, *Institutes of the Christian Religion*, ed. J. T. McNeill, trans. F. L. Battles, (Philadelphia, Pennsylvania: The Westminster Press, 1968). Calvin writes: "But God also designates himself by another special mark to distinguish himself more precisely from idols. For he so proclaims himself the sole God as to offer himself to be contemplated clearly in three persons. Unless we grasp these, only the bare and empty name of God flits about in our brains, to the exclusion of the true God." Bk. I, ch. XIII, 2, p.122

13. *Book of Confessions*, 8:20, 26, 27.

3

The Uselessness of the Church:
The Mysterious Gift of the Community of Faith

> Fear not, little flock, for it is your Father's good pleasure to give you the kingdom. Sell your possessions, and give alms; provide yourselves with purses that do not grow old, with a treasure in the heavens that does not fail, where no thief approaches and no moth destroys. For where your treasure is, there will your heart be also. Luke 12:32-34

It is somewhat ironic that many who might find language about God's uselessness offensive hardly stir when that same language is applied to the church. In fact, not much is expected of the church, and given its auxiliary function in much of the culture, its uselessness is simply assumed. The task, we often think, is how to make the church useful. After all, we live in a secular culture in which only very rarely is faith expected to contribute its insights on issues of public concern. The entertainment industry, for example, portrays a world almost entirely devoid of folk whose faith commitments are strong and vibrant. When was the last movie that portrayed the faith (or doubt, for that matter) of a believer struggling with the cost of discipleship? Do families in situation comedies ever go to church? Are there no prayers ever uttered on a soap opera? When a televangelist weeps on television and confesses that he has "sinned," his doing so is interpreted in every way except as a statement of faith. Of course, it may well not be, but to many in the culture, the fact that he can still describe himself as a "sinner" seems almost quaint and, in any case, is not taken seriously by a culture grown weary with "repentance." We have heard so many "confessions" before, from Presidents of the United States to million-dollar athletes, and now even the language of faith seems debased. No one doubts that it is still possible to sin, only that it is still possible to believe.

Eugene Peterson chronicles the depth of this unbelief, not by whining against a secular culture, but by pointing out the degree to which the church itself is implicated in it. "American pastors," he writes, "are abandoning their posts, left and right, and at an alarming rate. They are not leaving their churches and getting other jobs. Congregations still pay their salaries. Their names remain on the church stationery and they continue to appear in pulpits on Sundays. But they are abandoning their posts, their calling . . . . The pastors of America have metamorphosed into a company of shopkeepers, and the shops they keep are the churches. They are preoccupied with shopkeeper's concerns—how to keep the customers happy, how to lure customers away from down the street, how to package the goods so that the customers will lay out more money. . . . Some of them are very good shopkeepers. They attract a lot of customers, pull in great sums of money, develop splendid reputations. Yet it is still shopkeeping all the same. . . "[1]

No doubt many reasons could be given for the secularization of the culture, not all of them, by any means, lamentable. But as Stanley Hauerwas and William Willimon have suggested, the church trivializes itself when it accepts as its central business the providing of the culture with some kind of sacred canopy.[2] Indeed, nothing secularizes the church faster or more thoroughly than when it begins to interpret its own life in the light of its usefulness to the surrounding culture. And, yet, that is the inevitable result when the church ceases to struggle with the freedom of the triune God and, instead, contents itself with a god who will assist in a therapy or strategy of self-realization or when the church no longer defines itself in the light of Jesus Christ but sees in him only a model of a self-evident and self-evidently good humanity or when the church is unable to see anymore the ground of its own mysterious life in the freedom of the Father, Son, and Holy Spirit but, instead, understands itself as a redemption center where the customers are to be kept satisfied. The pursuit of happiness takes little notice of a church that does not recognize that the customer is always right. So, having long since found the freedom of God a tiresome thing and the Jesus of Scripture all too strange, the church finds itself lacking the strength even to see its own strangeness *over against the culture*, and so it can only become useful.

"Fear not little flock, for it is your Father's good pleasure to give you the kingdom." Part of the reason the church has such low expectations of itself is that it does not receive its own life as a gift from God. Indeed, if anything, the church tends to think of itself more often as a burden, if not an inheritance to be managed. To believe in God, even to accept Jesus Christ as Savior and Lord, seems not so difficult for many to do. But to confess that the church *is* the fruit of Christ's labors, the communion of his saints, the very place where the "manifold wisdom of God" is made known (Eph 3:10), that seems beyond us. We know better. We can, after all, *see* the church. We can see the hypocrisy of its virtues, the pettiness of its vices; we can see the failures of its hopes, the brokenness of its lives. Saints? Why, as Luther might have said, we don't even sin that well. At least the world is less pretentious; at least non-believers are more "honest"; at least a secular and pluralistic culture is not so hypocritical. Yes, we see all of that so well that talk of "the manifold wisdom of God" seems like so much pious rhetoric.

But do we see quite so well? Reinhold Niebuhr has often been quoted as saying that the one empirically verifiable doctrine of theology is the doctrine of human sinfulness. Sin seems so apparent, as apparent, in its way, as the weakness of the church. But to speak in this way of human sinfulness or the weakness of the church is to speak as if the whole matter were self-evident, and to speak in that way is, as we have seen, to miss the blinding scandal of the cross. If the sin of humanity or the weakness of the church is, after all, self-evident, then our problems are not really that intractable; in any case, they hardly require the intervention of the cross, only more education, more accurate perception, more acute sensitivity. *That* we can develop without having to receive our life from Another. For to receive our life from Jesus Christ, to believe in him, would mean to learn from him also what sin is, such that knowledge of sin would, far from being a self-evident thing, be a matter of faith.[3] Then the church's task would not be to apologize for its own sinfulness, but to discover it; not to be ashamed of its own weakness, but to learn of it; not to see, but to be blinded so that it can see what belongs to Christ.

What could be more useless than that? In a church that prides itself on spotting its own sin, no sin could possibly be greater than to be blind. But, strangely, in the New Testament it is not the sighted who see but the blind. The disciples, for example, see perfectly; they even see their own weaknesses (Mark 4:38; 9:28, 33-36); yet, seeing, they do not see. None of the gospels is more concerned with seeing than the gospel of John, which from the very first chapter ("we have beheld his glory") stresses seeing as an act of faith and, in fact, devotes the entire 9th chapter to the story of Jesus' healing of a man born blind. "Where is the sin?" his disciples ask, for they clearly see the man's blindness, and, obviously, such visible, awful blindness must be the result of sin. But Jesus replies, "It was not that this man sinned, or his parents, but that the works of God might be made manifest in him . . . As long as I am in the world, I am the light of the world." (John 9: 3, 5) What exactly is Jesus saying? Is he saying that the works of God will be manifest in the healing miracle about to take place? Or is he saying that the man was born blind and suffered this affliction the better to show off Jesus' therapeutic skills? Or could something else be going on here? Might not Jesus, in fact, be saying that the man's blindness is a kind of metaphor for the disciples' unbelief, a blindness of pharisaical self-evidence, such that the occasion of grace is not only or merely that the blind man sees but that Jesus, in bestowing

sight on the blind man, *reveals* the blindness of those who
supposedly see? It is apparently the work of the "light of
the world" to reveal to us our blindness, blindness which, in
fact, *cannot* see. In the story that is exactly what happens.
The blind man is given his sight by Jesus ("Whether he is a
sinner, I do not know; one thing I know, that though I was
blind, now I see." vs. 25) but the Pharisees, whose vision is
always 20/20, immediately doubt, and they doubt, not that
the blind man sees, but that he was ever blind! ("The Jews
did not believe that he had been blind. . . ." vs.18) It is the
blindness that Jesus reveals that truly scandalizes both dis-
ciple and Pharisee, though, in the end, it is not the blindness
Jesus criticizes but sight: "If you were blind, you have no
guilt; but now that you say 'We see,' your guilt remains"
(vs. 40).

Or take another example. No "conversion" is more
celebrated in the New Testament than that of the Apostle
Paul. But, in fact, what happens on the road to Damascus is
not that Paul is given improved eyesight so that he can see
better but, rather, that he is blinded, blinded by the light of
the world, a blindness which remains until that light,
through the hands of Ananias, opens his eyes again. "We
walk by faith not by sight" (2 Cor 5:7), Paul writes, not to
apologize for the church's dimness of vision but because
the blindness of faith actually *sees* better than self-evident
sight. That is why Paul adds, "We are of good courage" (vs.
8); that is, not because the church has such good vision; indeed, we are blind most of all to our own sinfulness—but
because through the gift of being blinded by the light of the
world, we are given to see Jesus (Heb 2:9).

At the heart of any conversion, C.S. Lewis writes, is
a blessed defeat.[4] If the church is to be converted from its
cynical despair and frantic usefulness, it must be blinded by
grace and learn from its blindness what it is to see. The
strange thing is that it takes faith to see, faith, especially, to
see one's own sinfulness, which is why the Apostles' Creed
never invites us to believe in sin as if it were a matter of
self-evidence, but, rather, to believe in the "forgiveness of
sins," that is, to believe in him who, in overcoming our sin,

reveals it. Apart from him, we do not see, and, most especially, we do not see our sin.

     If the church is not very interesting in its sinning to-
day, it is perhaps because the church does not have enough
faith to believe in its forgiveness. But, then, faith is a gift
that comes not at all naturally but from Jesus Christ himself, who, in touching our eyes, reveals that we have been
blind from birth, and never blinder than when we trust in
our own seeing rather than in his. Truly to see, then, is to be
given new eyes, eyes that see better than our own, eyes that
see what we cannot see, eyes that can see ourselves. And
where are such eyes? To see by faith is finally to trust in
Christ's seeing, his seeing *for* us, even through us; it is to
walk not as the blind are led by the blind ("And if a blind
man leads a blind man, both will fall into a pit." Matt
15:14) but as the blind are led by the light of the world.That
is how the church learns to see and learns to see not only its
own blindness but the blindness of all the useful saviors
who are only too glad to persuade us that our blindness is a
matter of self-evidence. It is not, but that it is not can only
be seen by faith.

     And that is also how the church learns to pray and
to work and to witness. We live in a world that desperately
wants to be told that it can see. That is the demand that always comes and threatens to turn the church of Jesus Christ
into a salvation shop. The lust to see, however, is always a
desire to see apart from Jesus Christ and, in that regard, has
hardly been confined to our day. Even at the beginning the
early church faced this threat. Then it was called "gnosticism," a religious effort to convince people that the only
thing standing between not seeing and seeing was their own
ignorance or even their self-evident sinfulness. By purify-
ing their sight, by training them to see better, by teaching
techniques of moral or religious purpose, the gnostics
promised to put their clients in the "know," a valuable place
to be which would separate them from the dullards who
simply could not "see." The attractiveness of this program
will be apparent to anyone who has ever watched a television commercial.[5] What is being sold is not toothpaste or

deodorant but, in fact, deliverance, deliverance from the horrible state of not-knowing, not even knowing that one has bad breath or that other people are talking. Compared to putting that anxiety to rest, the improvement in dental hygiene is merely an added benefit. (I believe this is why nothing seems to corrupt preaching quite like television; it is a medium for selling, and so often selling involves creating a need. "You got trouble, right here in River City." That is how trombones can be sold. And the gospel.)

In response to this highly popular and well-argued tradition of gnosticism, the church finally refused to play the salvation game. Instead, the church confessed. The church confessed Jesus Christ. Doctrinally, that meant that the church confessed that the Son of God incarnate in Jesus Christ was *of the same substance* with the Father (i.e., that in Jesus Christ we have to do with God, not information about him); secondly, the church confessed that in assuming human flesh, the Son of God assumed our *entire* humanity, not just part of it (i.e., that in Jesus Christ God redeems the entirety of our sinful nature, not just our bodies or souls or minds); and thirdly, the church confessed that faith in this God is itself a gift of the Holy Spirit, the Lord and Giver of life. The effect of all this theological struggle was to confess that the line that divides seeing from not seeing is not one that divides spiritual folk from more fleshly types, or moral athletes from the libertines, or people in the religious know from those who are not, but, rather, that divides Jesus Christ from everyone else. Spirituality puts us no closer to *seeing* Jesus; we are quite capable of turning spirituality into a means of our own self-realization. Our dilemma is that only the cross gives us eyes truly to see, and yet when we look at it, we are scandalized. Still, only there, as he is lifted up, does Jesus draw *all* to himself.

And that means that the church is not a group of especially gifted folk who are in the know, but, rather, the church is a community of faith "in which Jesus Christ acts presently as Lord in Word and Sacrament through the Holy Spirit." Only as such, then, is it also "the church of pardoned sinners" which "in the midst of a sinful world," is called "to testify with its faith as with its obedience, with its message as with its order, that it is solely his property and that it lives and wants to live solely from his comfort and from his direction."[6] What the church has to offer the world is not its knowledge, not even its salvation. The church has never saved anyone, a point our Reformed parents knew well and one that made them skeptical of serving up salvation to the culture as if it were a commodity. No, what the church has to offer the world is the only gift it has ever received: Jesus Christ. We should be clear about this. The gift which the church bears to the world is not a salvific condo in the south of France but a community that "sees" by being led around like a blind man by Jesus Christ, that is "saved" by being united to him, trusting that he will lead us where we are to go and into what we need to know. So it is that faith is really a trust in Jesus' seeing, in his praying, in his believing, in his dying, and in his living. That is what Paul called being a "slave to Christ," what Barmen confesses as being his "alone." And that is what enables the church to be free enough to be the church, even to rejoice in being the church, to live no more out of our own "seeing'" but out of the visible Word of God, Jesus Christ's own body and blood. That is why, again as Paul would remind us, "We are of good courage." We *are* of good courage. We are Christ's church, not by virtue of our secure grasp on him but by the grace of his unshakable grip on us. (" . . . and no one shall snatch them out of my hand." John 10:28). In light of such a gospel, the only sin could be trusting in our hands more than in those of Jesus Christ and, in fact, wanting a salvation apart from other sinners. Surely Jesus' grip cannot be that strong. Can it?

*   *   *   *   *

A Parable

In his book *The Brothers Karamazov,* Dostoyevsky

tells of a prostitute named Grushenka. She is passionately desired both by Fyodor, the father, and Dmitri, the oldest son. Grushenka, wiser than both, is, nevertheless, flattered by their attentions and amused by their antics. Still, her own eye is caught not by either one of these but by the youngest Karamazov, Alyosha, a monk who becomes a kind of Christ-figure in the book. One day, Alyosha is tricked into coming to visit the prostitute in her rooms. At first Grushenka considers seducing the young man, but soon, in spite of herself, finds that she is pouring out her soul to him. Alyosha does nothing; he merely listens. But he listens to her. Finally she confesses, "It's true, Alyosha, I had sly designs on you before. For I am a horrid, violent creature. But at other times I've looked upon you, Alyosha, as my conscience. I've kept thinking 'how anyone like that must despise a nasty thing like me!'" In an effort to explain herself, Grushenka tells Alyosha a parable.

The parable is about an old, mean-spirited woman who died and went to hell and there was plunged deep into a lake of fire. Her guardian angel goes to God on her behalf with the news that this old woman did one good deed in her whole life: she once pulled out an onion and gave it to an old beggar woman. And so God tells the angel to take the onion and hold it out to the woman in hell and pull her up. The angel does this, and the old woman grabs hold of the onion and slowly begins to emerge from the depths of hell. But when other inhabitants of that misery see that the woman is being pulled out, they rush to grab hold of her, and she, fearing that the onion will not be strong enough to pull everyone out, kicks them away. "I'm to be pulled out, not you. It's my onion," she says. And as soon as she says this, the onion does break, and they all fall back into hell.

Jesus Christ is the onion. He is the onion the church holds on to. We think that he is not strong enough to pull us all out of hell, especially if holding on to him *means* being held on to by other miserable creatures. To hold on to him, then, would be to risk our salvation. When we desire that salvation apart from Jesus Christ and what belongs to Jesus Christ or when we think the strength is in us and not finally

in his "good deed," then we are given what we want, and
we find the hell that awaits those who would prefer their
own salvation to the presence of Jesus Christ. The task of
the church is not to snatch at what we might lose or kick at
those we think have no right to hold on to us, but to hold on
to him who will not break and who will not save us without
pulling up a world of sinners by the strength of the cross.

Later, Grushenka turns to Alyosha and tells him, "I
have been waiting all my life for someone like you; I knew
someone like you would come and forgive me. I believed
that as nasty as I am, someone would really love me, not
only with a lustful love." And Alyosha, bending over her
and gently taking her head in his hands, replies, "What
have I done to you? I only gave you an onion. . . . "[7]

*   *   *   *   *

That is why the church's efforts to become useful to
a suspicious culture are bound, in the end, to be comical,
rather like trying to convince people that singing in the
shower is, in fact, operatic fare. When we are told, or when
we discover that it is not, we are disappointed and often try
to cover our nakedness (to mix a metaphor) with strategi-
cally placed fig leaves. We think the hard part of the faith is
convincing the world of the strength of our grasp on Jesus
Christ, when, in fact, the world, often wiser than the children of light, remains unconvinced. But what is scandalously hard for us to believe is the strength of Jesus Christ's grip
on us. That we find difficult. Yet that is the heart of the
gospel. "Who shall *separate* us from the love of Christ?"
(Rom 8:35). Our problem is not how we can find this God
and help the world find him too, but, rather, how we can escape him. The world's destiny, Paul says, is to *be* found. Indeed, it has already been found in Jesus Christ. That is why
he calls us "more than conquerors," because it is "through
him who loved us." That is what we are called to believe,
not that "I found it!" but the much more scandalous and,
finally, much more joyful news, that the world *has con-*

quered in Jesus Christ. The church is the place where the world hears of its conquest and where we learn to celebrate that reality, where we learn to sing and practice our notes for a chorus that will one day join the heavenly host in a never-ending "Alleluia." The task is not to believe that we are operatic virtuosos, but to learn the song and begin to sense how it carries us, even us, into the kingdom.

Dorothy L. Sayers once wrote that God suffered three great humiliations: the first was becoming flesh; the second was dying in that flesh; and the third was entrusting that story to the church.[8] The third humiliation may be the greatest one of all, since we are so tempted to improve on the gospel of love and turn it into something really useful. But when has love ever been useful? Which of us, in raising our children, waits until they grow up, get good jobs, and behave themselves before deciding to love them? What marriage can survive mere utility? Love, as William Willimon notes,[9] does not get to choose; it does not even get to choose whom to love. Rather, it is chosen. Who, after all, chooses to fall in love with a drug addict or an alcoholic or a bankrupt? No one. Most alcoholics are sober when we marry them; most drug addicts are beautiful babies when we give birth to them; most bankruptcies are due to unforeseen developments. Who chooses to have a Down's child or one with leukemia? No one. But those are the gifts we receive. The great myth is that love is always free to choose. Love, in fact, is never free to choose; it reveals itself, instead, as love when all the choices have already been made, when it's sickness rather than health, poorer rather than richer, death rather than life. Love is what never ends.

Which is why love can never finally be merely useful, only essential. Without it we die. And that is why the church's real gift to the world is not Jesus Christ in abstraction but Jesus Christ in a concrete form, Jesus Christ living as community.[10] The way we learn about love is not telling the world how to do it (as if the gospel were some kind of lecture) but living as the community of Jesus Christ, *whom we have not chosen to love but who, for his own purpose, has chosen to love us.* The church is the place where, in the

fellowship of Jesus Christ, we learn to love those whom we
have not chosen but who are presented to us as a gift: our
parents, our friends, the stranger, even our enemies. The
church is not called to do anything for the world but to be
that community of faith that believes that in Jesus Christ it
is the world that conquers, that believes that in Jesus Christ
it is the world that cannot escape his love.

There are three immediate implications for the
church in this strange gospel. The first is that, in light of the
inseparability of Jesus Christ and sinful humanity, the most
pressing task before the church is to receive itself as a gift
of that Lord and claim that inseparability. We are called, I
believe, to *love* the church, not to take it for granted, not to
bemoan its institutional failings, not to long for its institutional success, not even to cultivate the virtue of a prophet-
ic loneliness, but to cultivate the vineyard God has given
us, to confess that in the church's worship and work, God
cultivates us. We ought not to call common what God has
cleansed. Implied in this love for the church is also a love
for what belongs to the church: to cultivate its worship, to
offer there our best, to love its preaching and honor it as the
bread of life, to love its fellowships and sacraments as the
sign of God's inseparable fellowship with us. Note well: I
do not intend by this invitation to love the church as a therapeutic technique in esteem-building, nor do I imply a con-
tentment with the status quo that wishes only that believers
would concentrate on the positive side of things. The
church's present condition is, in my judgement, wretched
and poor, its resources in faith beyond the capability of
therapy to restore. For the church to receive its own life in
love means nothing more than to receive it from the hand
of God, that is, to receive it as something of value because
he has called us to be a part of it. The question is, do we
love the church enough to struggle for its soul? To expect
to hear from its mouth the Word of God? To sense in its
wretchedness the judgment and redemption of its Lord?
There is no shame in struggling to point to the mysterious
and wondrous reality that beggars our words, that reveals
our failings precisely as the church of Jesus Christ. Indeed,

throughout history the church has *thrived* on such failings. There is only shame in succeeding, in succeeding by pointing to a much less demanding reality, a reality that is conventional and clear and useful. Then we will have failed in the only thing that truly matters, that is, in rendering our own witness to that marvelous grace of God that always does more than we can ask or think.

Secondly, the church is not called to undertake missions but to be in mission. By that I mean that the greatest witness the church can make against racism is not to become politically (or theologically) correct or to fund interest groups who are, but, to put it bluntly, to worship, pray, and live together in communities of faith. That means, concretely, that the church's task is to start new congregations and redevelop other ones as communities which, as a result of their faith in the gospel of Jesus Christ, do not take racial divisions as the ultimate word about human life and whose refusal to do so is not merely "in principle" but is embodied in their life together. That is hard work. That is especially hard work in a culture that has grown used to taking its own lines of racial division more seriously than the gospel. The rhetoric of liberation, like the rhetoric of white supremacy, has hardened the lines and made it more difficult to see what is *ours* in Christ. Instead of challenging the heresy of separation in the name of the inseparability of all sinners in the love of Christ (and doing so by building communities of faith, not by passing resolutions), the church has largely retreated from such a daunting prospect, preferring to let the communities of culture, race, and class have the field. It is really not that difficult to fund an ethnic heritage center. The challenge is to build a church, a church whose gospel calls into question the "certainties" of every culture, even the culture of the church. And, yet, it is that gospel that is tough enough to withstand our divisions and our failures; tough enough even to withstand our hatred and our pride; tough enough, in fact, to lead us to the cross no one chooses but which is the only true basis for human community. The task before the church of Jesus Christ, then, is to build churches that witness to his lordship.

Thirdly, in addition to celebrating its life and sharing its life, the church is called to receive from Jesus Christ the discipline of its life. The love of Christ is costly; there is nothing cheap about it. Unlike the therapies of salvation, union with Christ is both a humiliation and an exaltation. "Only in America" would we think of setting out on the journey of faith as if we would never find ourselves with an army behind us and a sea in front of us or as if we could get through the wasteland of our own culture without hungering and thirsting for some real food, as if the promised land were "retirement'" or "making it'" or being famous for fifteen minutes. Americans, said F. Scott Fitzgerald, believe in the green light. And so we do. But the pursuit of the green light kills. It turns the pilgrimage of faith into an amusement park of cheap, but utterly predictable and safe, salvation. And the result is that the church no longer wants to be the church but, rather, "the fellowship of excitement."[11]

In fact, the life the church receives from its Lord is not a life of cheap thrills but of disciplined courage. It takes courage to walk through the desert, just as it takes courage to walk in our cities' streets. It takes courage to walk into someone's broken marriage or to live in the hell of someone's terminal cancer. It takes courage, most of all, to believe that in the midst of this *mess* God is at work shaping my life and yours into its true Christ-like form. How does one find such courage? There are no quick or easy techniques, which is enough to give most of us trouble with the gospel right off the bat. The problem is that there are no long or painful techniques either. What there is is bread. What there is is wine. What there is is the regular worship of God, where his word is eaten up by hungry and lonely and cowardly sinners. How does one find courage to live as Christ's in this world? I am not sure that I am qualified to speak, but this I know, such courage is not found apart from his discipling presence, apart from the stamina of his spirit, the work of his love. Only in his company do we learn to be disciples; only in his way do we dare to be the church.

NOTES

1. Eugene Peterson, *Working the Angles*, (Grand Rapids: Eerdmans, 1988), p. 1.

2. Stanley Hauerwas and William Willimon, *Resident Aliens*, (Nashville: Abingdon, 1989), pp. 22ff. "The theologian's job is not to make the gospel credible to the modern world, but *to make the world credible to the gospel*." (p.24) The phrase "sacred canopy" is, of course, from the title of Peter Berger's book, *The Sacred Canopy*, (Garden City: Doubleday, 1968). In describing the *Kulturprotestantismus* which was the legacy of Schleiermacher's "eternal covenant" between the church and culture, Berger writes: "In other words, the theological enterprise now takes place with constant regard for a reference group of secular intellectuals—precisely the 'cultured despisers' of religion. . . . *They* rather than the sources of his own tradition, now serve the Protestant theologian as arbiters of cognitive acceptability." p.158. Berger is keenly aware of the way liberal Protestantism was (is?) quite willing to bargain away its faith (i.e., to render it useful to the culture) in exchange for approbation and even power within that culture. In fact, the more faith orients itself toward organizing the culture, the less it has to apologize for as *faith*. Berger makes the intriguing observation that Kierkegaard, for example, who was not interested in Liberal Protestantism's program of usefulness but who rather wished only to make things more difficult, remained "marginal to the theological situation" in the 19th century, and only came into his own "after the end of the Schleiermachian era." p.159

3. Karl Barth, *Church Dogmatics* IV/1, ed. G.W. Bromiley and T.F. Torrance, (Edinburgh: T. & T. Clark, 1961), p. 390: "But this knowledge of real sin takes place in the knowledge of Jesus Christ. Why in this knowledge? . . . Because the God against whom the man of sin contends has judged this man, and therefore myself as this man, in the self-offering and death of Jesus Christ His own Son, putting him

to death and destroying him. . . .We are all wearers of the old garment which was taken off and destroyed." That is at least the beginning of the reason that Barth maintains that knowledge of sin must first of all be knowledge of Jesus Christ.

4. Cited in Ralph Wood, *The Comedy of Redemption*, (Notre Dame, Indiana: Univ. of Notre Dame Press, 1987), p. 118.

5. Neil Postman, *The Disappearance of Childhood*, (New York: Delacorte Press, 1982), pp. 108-115.

6. *The Book of Confessions*, (Louisville, Kentucky: General Assembly, Presbyterian Church (U.S.A.)), 8:26.8:27.

7. Fyodor Dostoyevsky, *The Brothers Karamazov*, trans by Constance Garrett, (Signet Classic, 1980), pp. 315-329.

8. Cited in "When Rain Spatters the Window," a review of *Disappointment With God: Three Ouestions No One Asks Aloud*, (by Philip Yancey, Grand Rapids, Zondervan, 1988), by Jack Roeda in *The Reformed Journal*, Vol. 39, No. 4, (April 1989): p. 28.

9. William Willimon, "The People We're Stuck With" in *The Christian Century*, (October 17, 1990): pp. 924-925.

10. Dietrich Bonhoeffer, *Christ the Center*, trans. by John Bowden, (New York: Harper & Row, 1966;), "Christ as Community," pp. 59-61. Cf. also Bonhoeffer's dissertation *The Communion of the Saints*, trans. R. Gregor Smith, (New York: Harper & Row, 1963), pp. 103-114.

11. Cf. "Megachurches Strive To Be All Things To All Parishioners" under Gustav Niebuhr's by-line, in *The Wall St. Journal*, (May 13, 1991).

4

The Uselessness Of Preaching

PSALM 2

Why do the nations conspire,
   and the peoples plot in vain?
The kings of the earth set themselves
   and the rulers take counsel together,
   against the Lord and his anointed, saying,
"Let us burst their bonds asunder, and cast
   their cords from us."

He who sits in the heavens laughs;
   the Lord has them in derision.
Then he will speak to them in his wrath,
   and terrify them in his fury, saying,
"I have set my king on Zion, my holy hill."
I will tell of the decree of the Lord:
   He said to me, "You are my son, today I
   have begotten you.
Ask of me, and I will make the nations your heri-
   tage, and the ends of the earth your possession.
You shall break them with a rod of iron,
   and dash them in pieces like a potter's vessel."

Now therefore, O kings, be wise;
   be warned, O rulers of the earth.

Serve the Lord with fear,
  with trembling kiss his feet,
  lest he be angry, and you perish in the way;
  for his wrath is quickly kindled.

Blessed are all who take refuge in him.

In Flannery O'Connor's short story "The Enduring Chill," there is a wonderful encounter between a frustrated writer, sick with undulant fever, and an Irish priest called to the house to bless the young man in preparation for last rites. The writer, who, though sick, is not sick unto death, wants a Jesuit to come, a man of culture who will appreciate the pathos and the absurdity of an artist's dying young. What he gets, however, is a common priest, whose main interest in coming is to shrive the young man's soul, to bring him to a saving knowledge of Jesus Christ. Since the priest, Father Finn, is from Ireland, the writer, Asbury Fox, asks him what he thinks of Joyce.

"Joyce who?" replies the priest.

"James Joyce," Asbury said and laughed.

The priest brushed his huge hand in the air as if he were bothered by gnats. "I haven't met him," he said. "Now. Do you say your morning and night prayers?"

Asbury appeared confused. "Joyce was a great writer," he murmured . . .

"You don't, eh?" said the priest. "Well, you will never learn to be good unless you pray regularly. You cannot love Jesus unless you speak to Him."

"The myth of the dying god has always fascinated me," Asbury shouted, but the priest did not appear to catch it.

"Do you have trouble with purity?" he demanded, and as Asbury paled, he went on without waiting for an answer. "We all do but you must pray to the Holy Ghost for it. Mind, heart and body. Nothing is overcome without prayer. Pray with your family. Do you pray with your family?"

"God forbid," Asbury answered. "My mother doesn't have time to pray and my sister is an atheist," he shouted.

"A shame!" said the priest. "Then you must pray for them."

"The artist prays by creating," Asbury ventured.

"Not enough!" snapped the priest. "If you do not pray daily, you are neglecting your immortal soul. Do you know your catechism?"

"Certainly not," Asbury muttered.

"Who made you?" the priest asked in a martial tone.

"Different people believe different things about that," Asbury said.

"God made you," the priest said shortly. "Who is God?"

"God is an idea created by man," Asbury said, feeling that he was getting into stride, that two could play at this.

"God is a spirit, infinitely perfect," the priest said. "You are a very ignorant boy. Why did God make you?"

"God didn't . . . "

"God made you to know Him, to love Him, to serve Him in this world and to be happy with Him in the next!" the old priest said in a battering voice. "If you don't apply yourself to the catechism, how do you expect to know how to save your immortal soul?"

Asbury saw he had made a mistake and that it was time to get rid of the old fool. "Listen," he said, "I'm not a Roman."

"A poor excuse for not saying your prayers!" the old man snorted.

Asbury slumped slightly on the bed. "I'm dying," he shouted.

"But you are not dead yet!" said the priest. . . . "God does not send the Holy Ghost to those who don't ask for Him. Ask Him to send the Holy Ghost."

"The Holy Ghost?" Asbury said.

"Are you so ignorant you've never heard of the Holy Ghost?" the priest asked.

"Certainly I've heard of the Holy Ghost," Asbury said

furiously, "and the Holy Ghost is the last thing I'm looking
for!"

"And he may be the last thing you get," the priest
said. . . .[1]

The comedic aspects of this encounter are only part-
ly due to the incongruity in expectations of both artist and
priest: the former prepared to discuss aesthetics with a cul-
tivated and perhaps worldly student of religion, the latter
prepared to offer catechetical instruction to a dying soul.
The misunderstanding is funny. However, O'Connor's hu-
mor, like so many of her stories, does more than make us
laugh. The priest's stubbornly simple faith is scandalously
embarrassing in a world that cannot quite take it seriously,
that cannot believe that it is real. A useless superstition, it is
best left behind as a childish habit which one outgrows. In
its place one discovers more useful explanations: the myth
of the dying god, for example, or the creative mythologiz-
ing of a James Joyce. These "explanations" have a way of
rendering a world to us without cost, of enriching us without discomfort. They can be accepted or rejected, but at
least they do not call for faith. They have the advantage of
keeping the world and God at arm's length, permitting talk
"about" such matters but drawing the line at any kind of in-
volvement in which we might be judged or any kind of
power to which we might owe allegiance.

Even the gospel itself is a candidate for such a
translation into usefulness. Earlier in the story, Asbury re-
members being in New York and attending a lecture on Ve-
danta Hinduism in the company of a Jesuit named Ignatius
Vogle, a fellow-traveller in the pursuit of religious enlightenment. In response to a question concerning the apparent
nihilism of the lecturer's point of view, the Jesuit deliber-
ately eschews any words that might voice the central claim
of the Christian faith and, instead, opines weakly that there
is "a real probability of the New Man, assisted, of course,
by the Third Person of the Trinity." This "explanation" is
quite acceptable to Asbury, who, after all, is willing to be-

lieve almost anything so long as it will "assist" him in some form of self-realization but, in any case, not in such a way that would embarrass his dignity or contradict his self-understanding or challenge his soul. Asbury, as Ralph Wood notes, has no trouble with a God who is willing to remain abstract. Such a god is, in fact, quite useful in his "assistance."[3]

But it is precisely the unabstract reality of God's judgment with which Father Finn is dealing. His faith is thought useless by Asbury until it is found to be dangerous. And it becomes dangerous only when Finn confronts Asbury with the claim of that faith on the young man's life. Then, and only then, does Asbury *confess* what he truly believes, namely, that "the Holy Ghost is the last thing I'm looking for," and in that confession he comes close to speaking authentically for the first time, both of himself and of God.

Finn's outrageous presentation of the gospel of Jesus Christ actually enables Asbury to leave his hard-won alienation behind and enter a community, albeit a community of sinners, in the simple and truthful confession that the Holy Spirit is the last thing any of us is looking for. Finn's acknowledgement that grace is not what we are looking for but what we get sounds more like a word of judgment than a piece of good news, and it is true that in this story the descent of the Spirit resembles more an ice pick than it does a dove. "How can the Holy Ghost fill your soul when it's full of trash?" the priest finally asks Asbury. "The Holy Ghost will not come until you see yourself as you are—a lazy ignorant conceited youth!"[4]

Such a vision is terrifying, especially to those whose alienation from the earthiness of the gospel is such an article of faith. To them, the ice pick of the Holy Spirit threatens to wound even as it chips away at their certainties. What Father Finn knows that Asbury doesn't is that the gospel is precisely about power. It is this knowledge that reverses the positions of sophisticate and man of faith, making the former seem naive and the latter utterly realistic. For Asbury thinks that the gospel is finally harmless, something that can be discussed and appreciated, measured and put to work, and all without losing control. Finn is under no such illusion. He knows that faith in Jesus Christ means precisely to be defeated, to be scandalized to the core of one's being, leaving one helpless save for the severe mercy of the cross. The gift that he gives Asbury through his catechizing is the sense of the power struggle involved, the sense of danger the gospel represents. It is Asbury's awakening to that danger that occasions his outburst about not looking for the Holy Spirit. Even here, however, he has no idea how dangerous the Spirit might be, unaware as he is that the Spirit is looking for him.[5]

Asbury Fox is a modern gnostic, a recognizable type who like their ideas pure, untainted by the vicissitudes of history or the foibles of the flesh. Unable to take seriously the world as it presents itself, and a bit ashamed of its crude physicality, such gnostics deal with an intractable situation by trying to think their way out of it. That is all that needs to be done, after all. The problem is in our minds or in our world-views, in our language or attitudes. Like the gnostics of old, we find ourselves in an alien world, the true formula for the understanding of which seems to be just out of reach. In this world God never quite becomes flesh. He does not have to. Rather, God, as some metaphysical abstraction, reconciles the world to himself within our own minds and there gives us a glimpse of his perfection. All we need to do is to attain that level of enlightenment, that gnosis, which will put us through to such a vision. Then God will have become useful indeed.

But why, as Gerhard Forde asks, if this account is true, "did God go to all the bother to be in Christ to reconcile the world to himself? Why the suffering, agony, and death on the cross?"[6] Why, as St. Anselm notes, did the Almighty have to "stoop to such lowly things" or "do anything with such great labor"?[7] If Asbury is right, such stooping was useless, even shameful for God to do. And yet, Asbury's modesty here on behalf of God is entirely false, for it conceals his own conviction that there is no sin so great that we cannot think our way out of it, no evil so radical that would require the intervention of God. And perhaps most devastating of all, such modesty implies that there is no human life so significant that it would require the grace of the cross.

That is what makes Father Finn's catechizing so threatening to Asbury; it threatens to expose him as a child of God, as a sinner of Christ's own redeeming. Asbury thinks he can only be interesting if he has achieved a certain level of gnosis. That is why his relationships are not really relationships at all but poses, matters of attitude and ideas. A relationship in which he is known by Another, who is not impressed with such poses but who is faithful to the image of grace that, in fact, is Asbury, that is almost too frightening for Asbury to consider. He can only call it useless because to take it seriously would shatter, not his ideas about God, but his life. And if Asbury clings to any article of faith, it is that a shattered life is a life that has ceased to be interesting, for it is a life that has admitted defeat, a life that is carrying around a wound within itself that ideas and attitudes and poses cannot heal. That that is precisely the nature of his own illness is, of course, the pivot of the story, a pivot, however, that comes to light most clearly only in the catechizing of Father Finn.

Indeed, Father Finn's catechetical work does what good preaching ought to do; namely, it renders our lives visible in the light of the cross. For only the cross is strong enough to pierce through our poses, and only the cross is rude enough to reveal our contrivances for avoiding the truth. Fearing its power, we seek to reduce and trivialize it by reducing and trivializing our world and its mystery. O'Connor herself identified this move with liberal Protestantism, a school of faith which held "'that man has never fallen, never incurred guilt, and is ultimately perfectible by his own efforts. Therefore evil in this light is a problem of better housing, sanitation, health etc. and all the mysteries will eventually be cleared up."[8] "What people don't realize," she once wrote to a friend, "is how much religion costs. They think faith is a big electric blanket, when of course it is the cross."[9]

The gospel is that *the* most interesting thing about Asbury Fox is that he is a sinner. It is precisely his opposition to grace that renders his life significant; it is precisely his withdrawal from the human community that bespeaks his embarrassment with being a part of a community of sinners; it is precisely his efforts to reduce suffering itself to a pose that reveals the emptiness of his own convictions. And yet none of this is self-evident. It is only as grace confronts him that Asbury opposes it and so is revealed; only as grace seeks him out in the form of parent, neighbor and priest that his withdrawal gains strength; it is only as he is confronted by the blunt claims of the cross that he is momentarily lifted out of his posturing into an authentic expression of godlessness.

And in that, of course, he comes very close to the gospel. something, I suspect, Miss O'Connor knew very well, but which remains a difficult thing for preachers to grasp. To be sure, very few of us write as well or as perceptively as Flannery O'Connor, but what is at stake in this extended parable is not the artist's narrative abilities so much as her dogmatic and even homiletic insights.

*   *   *   *   *

The gospel, when it is preached, is heard as a word of power that threatens our deepest and most cherished convictions concerning who is in control of this world. A sermon that does not challenge other gods in the name of the God of Jesus Christ is not a sermon worthy of his name.

The gospel, when it is preached, is heard as a word of grace that threatens our deepest and most certain convictions about the power of evil and the futility of hope. A sermon that does not confront us with the resurrection of Jesus Christ as the ground for our hope, above all, in ourselves, is not a sermon worthy of his name.

The gospel, when it is preached, is a word of joy that laughs at the pretense of what we are well-schooled to take seriously, directing us not to an explanation that "explains it all" for us, but to a deepening mystery that cannot be fathomed by any of our explanations, and most certainly not by our religious ones.

A sermon that knows neither the laughter of the divine comedy nor the embarrassment of being beggared by such a mystery is not a sermon worthy of the gospel of Jesus Christ.

$$\ast \quad \ast \quad \ast \quad \ast \quad \ast$$

The gospel is a word of power that threatens us. One might argue that to speak of the threatening word of the gospel first is to misconstrue that gospel from the beginning. The first word of the gospel is, as Karl Barth reminds us, not a word of law but of grace: "Fear not!" Why, then, should one begin by speaking of preaching as a threatening word? Is this not a return to those kinds of games where the preacher first of all tries to convince his hearers that they have "trouble in River City" and then, and only then, brings the gospel in as a kind of solution? American religion is well-acquainted with this kind of game already. What makes it a game and, therefore, a trivialization of the gospel is not just its beginning point but, rather, its assumption that it knows already, in advance of having heard the gospel, so to speak, what, in fact, opposes the gospel and thinks, therefore, that it can begin with the self-evident truths of whatever it is that is "troubling River City." But, of course, that means that the tail is wagging the dog, that is, that the gospel is not needed to discern such troubles and that, in fact, it is *only* the "answer" to them. So it is that the gospel is defined in the light of our self-understanding and is found to be useful as it fits into our world, as it becomes an "answer" we can use.

Which means, of course, that the gospel is rendered harmless. No, what threatens us is not the possibility that the gospel might contain some negative news about our

world. That we can deal with. That we can even turn into
therapies of redemption, occasions for "feeling better"
about ourselves. No, what threatens us is the possibility that
the gospel cannot be fitted into our world, that we cannot
turn it to good use, cannot make of it even an "answer,"
that, in fact, it undermines our world and our place in it.
What threaten us is the fact that the gospel *embarrasses* us
in its refusal to be used and, even more, in its shameless
willingness to use us. What we find frightening is the power of the gospel, its overthrowing of our world, of our convictions, of our powers. What we fear is the embarrassment
of poverty, of weakness, of hunger, of emptiness. We will
do anything to hide these embarrassing truths from ourselves and others. We will even turn the gospel into a game
of religious options to keep from having to deal with this
threat.

There is, of course, nothing self-evident about this
threat. It is seen only in the gospel. But there it is seen well
enough: in the rich young ruler's embarrassed turning away
at the vision of his true poverty; in Peter's embarrassed refusal to let Jesus wash his feet; in Israel's and the church's
embarrassment over the rather weak rationale for God's
choosing of them to be his people (e.g., "It was not because
you were more in number than any other people that the
Lord set his love upon you. . . ." Deut.7:7. "For consider
your call; not many of you were wise according to worldly
standards, not many powerful . . . . " 1 Cor. 1:26) The threat
with which both Israel and the church are confronted is precisely the possibility that, in not being able to "answer,"
much less "explain" why it is that God has chosen them,
they will seek such "answers" and "explanations" in themselves. Scripture is the witness to God's faithfulness in shat-
tering these idolatrous "answers" and "explanations" in his
shameless giving of himself as the ground for our understanding. So it is that both Israel and the church can only
confess what they know to be true; they can only point to
that One in whom they are chosen, and in him discover a
world which has already been chosen for love even before
its foundations were laid.

But to confess that is precisely not to offer a rationale for it. And that is hard. For it is to be empty when the
world expects us to be full. And so, embarrassed by our
emptiness, we, too, look for reasons to justify this choice. It
must be because we are rich or successful or "privileged" or
possess the most liberating ideology or are truly virtuous.
That must be the reason. And so we preach the "good
news" of our strength and fullness, even the power of our
marginalization, and are never threatened by the gospel embarrassment of our emptiness, and even death, that is revealed only in Jesus Christ. God, we think, is no different
from other goals in life, and if reasons are wanting, then
reasons can be found.

But, in fact, God *reveals* himself to be unlike our
idols precisely in his refusal to be some religious goal, even
a self-evidently worthy one. Indeed, it is the fact that we
cannot *reveal* God, that we have to *wait upon* God to reveal
himself, that overturns our world. To preach the gospel in
ignorance of this fact is to assume that the "good news" is
something we can reveal, name, identify, and claim, which
is to say, it is to preach something that is not the gospel of
Jesus Christ. But this God names himself and constitutes in
his own giving what the gospel gift is to be. He identifies
himself as Father, Son, and Holy Spirit and creates out of
his own life the space for us to receive this gift. It is a gift
which, indeed, is good but whose goodness defines itself
even as it shatters our notion of good. It is a gift that, from
its first entrance into the world, threatened entrenched cen-
ters of power, from Herod to "all in Jerusalem with him." It
is a gift that threatens us today, such that to proclaim it
means to take a position *against* what is self-evidently obvious, useful, and benevolent. The proclamation of this gift
entails the "arrogant" presupposition that the world does
not know what it is talking about when it speaks generally
of goodness or truth or beauty, not to mention faith, hope,
and love, *until* it has been addressed by the word of the gospel. In this sense, preaching is *antagonistic*; it knows itself
to be engaged in a cause that opposes the world's claim to
self-sufficiency. Indeed, preaching, rather than moderating

this struggle, heightens it and renders it visible.

It is this sense of the *difficulty* of preaching that is missing from so many pulpits today. Unfortunately, for many, preaching is not difficult. It is easy, useful, a way for us to sort out what is politically correct or therapeutically helpful. Another way of saying the same thing is merely to note that no one is embarrassed by the impossibility of preaching today, just as very few are arrogant enough to believe that it is the occasion for a power struggle between the gospel and the culture in which we live. Unlike Scripture, where the cost of that struggle is laid bare on every page, a preacher today is loath to begin by assuming that what has to be said will have to be said in opposition to the culture's effort to define the terms. But, then, Scripture is confident, whereas we are not. Scripture tells stories in which a future for God's people is envisioned and unfolded in its own word, which then engages the culture. We, on the other hand, sense that Scripture is too weak for that and so must be "explained" in terms of something more powerful: an ideology, a metaphor, a way of life, such that the more our sermons "explain," the less confident they become.

Preaching which takes its starting point in the gospel will begin by assuming that the word it has to say will contradict the culture, that it will surprise. Such an assumption is not a pose, for, in fact, the gospel attests in every place the unexpected nature of grace, whether it is found on a rock pillow in Bethel or on the road to Emmaus. Those who believe are those who have been, in a very real sense, ambushed by grace. And such preaching surprises the culture most of all when it dissents from the prevailing view of the culture's self-sufficiency. Even dissent is surprising to the kingdoms of this world. How could anyone question the "American Way of Life"? That is why preaching is a subversive activity and never more so than when it leads to the praise of God. There is nothing more subversive in our world than doxology, for joy and gladness in the praise of God deprive the powers of this world of the solemn allegiance which they think is their due and undermine their claims to self-sufficiency. A sermon should begin, then, by recognizing its subversive character; by venturing, in the name of faith, some skepticism about the self-sufficiency of the world; by risking the embarrassment of not fitting into a tidy and well-made world. The gospel that begins in a rather cold and dirty stable and ends in the dereliction of the cross will not be offended by such untidiness; rather, it will find itself quite at home there.

*   *   *   *   *

But the gospel does not just give us a place to stand so that we can dissent from the prevailing culture; it also gives us a place to go. The other side of the culture's self-worship is its deep despair, its profound conviction that we are alone and isolated, powerless to do anything, and helpless in our loneliness. We live in a world where we have no trouble envisioning ourselves surrounded by frightening beasts: racial conflict, AIDS, illicit drugs, crime, war, family disintegration. The resources our culture gives us for combatting these beasts are pitifully small. The best we can seem to do is to declare "war" on them, because war strikes us as the only metaphor ultimate enough to engage the popular imagination and achieve the social cohesiveness for dealing with such issues. War invites sacrifice, we think, and compels unselfish behavior. But war has its casualties, and in the absence of any sense of shared convictions, a society at war with these great beasts soon finds in the war itself a kind of self-justifying metaphor for its own life. So it is that the relationships society engenders between people are no longer founded on communities of faith or nurture, or even shared convictions or interests, but on the increasingly harsh laws and regulations mandated by the need to defeat the enemy. And as a result society begins to resemble more and more Thomas Hobbes' view of the state of nature, namely, life that is "solitary, poor, nasty, brutish and short."

A society of "free agents," bristling in the defense of their rights and suspicious of the encroachments of others, will be disconcerted, if not baffled, by a community in which freedom is defined in terms of the cross; where the most difficult task is not defending what one has but believing that one is forgiven; where life together is not the burden we bear but the point of life itself.

To preach the gospel is to lift up this community of faith, and to lift it up, not as a noble thing to do in troublous times, but as the very content of the gospel itself. Because we have thought for so long that the gospel was an "explanation" of the world, we have thought that understanding it was primarily a matter of the mind or heart or disposition or attitude. Accordingly, one might be quite religious without having any use for the church. America, of course, is, if not the birthplace of this point of view, at least its best illustration. And, as a result, religion in America has often exacerbated the myth of the individual communing with God rather than calling it into question. Moreover, given the widespread acceptance of Christianity as an "explanation" of the world, the *idea* of Christianity can survive only at the cost of limiting the embarrassment of any instance of the idea in history. For as long as Christianity seeks to justify itself as an idea, one possible idea among others, then one need not bother overmuch about the community of faith, and certainly not the local congregation. The universal is the norm; the particular, but an instance.

But, in fact, as Lesslie Newbigin has shown, the scandal of particularity is at the heart of the gospel, just as it is at the heart of the community of faith.[10] What denies the church's affirmation of Jesus Christ as God incarnate also threatens the church's claim to be part of that gospel, a threat made more visible by the scandalous particularity of the local congregation. At least since the Enlightenment, it has not been difficult to argue that Jesus, far from being the particular and unique instance within history of the self-revelation of God, was, instead, a religious teacher, who, perhaps to a greater degree than most, was inspired but who was, nevertheless, a man like the rest of us. In a world where we can know only phenomena, there are no exceptions, or, as Lessing might remind us, there is no one to help us over the ditch between necessary truths of reason (or faith) and accidental truths of history. Moreover, there is something almost arrogant, so it is often argued, about the singularity of the gospel. Why the Jews? Why, of all people, this first century Palestinian rabbi? Why the church? Isn't God available to us all? "Modern historical consciousness" demands that we abandon claims to Christ's uniqueness, even as it informs us that such claims are themselves culturally conditioned.[11]

Whether "modern historical consciousness" is able to sustain its critical role in the absence of some faith claims of its own is, of course, another question, but underlying its critique of the truth claims of faith is more than a hint of moral and intellectual exhaustion. Nevertheless, what is at stake here is a view of truth that can be known by a neutral observer; known without being known. But it is the claim of faith, not just that we know, but, above all, that we are known; that to know God is to enter into a communion, indeed, into the divine life in which the knowledge of this particular God revealed in Jesus Christ *includes* life and worship in a particular community of faith. "Only in America," one might say, has it become possible to separate our life in Christ from life in Christ's church, a separation having much to do with our own Enlightenment legacy. The point is, however, that the proclamation of the gospel contradicts our culture at no more vulnerable point than when it insists that Jesus Christ is simply not available to us apart from his *body*, that is, the church. The scandal of particularity is never more embarrassing than when it directs us to the local congregation, i.e., to the difficult, small, fleshly, community of faith.

And this is so, not just because the gospel raises some uncomfortable questions to our belief in the neutrality of the individual but, more, because the gospel affirms that, just as there is a community of persons in the triune God, each indwelling the other, and just as there is a community of the cross, in which Jesus Christ refuses even in death to be without sinful humanity, so there is within us a completion that is known only in the life of the other. "Hell is other people" could have been said only by someone offended by the intrusion of God into an otherwise solitary kingdom. To be healed from the effects of that lie is to be found at a banquet: dethroned yet welcomed, impoverished yet happy, surrounded yet convivial. Though there is nothing about which our world is more skeptical than a happy ending, the gospel is insistent upon nothing less, and it is a happiness that is precisely other people, indeed, other sinners bound together in Jesus Christ.

A sermon proclaims this congregational life at its very heart, or it has nothing to say to our world. That this is news (and not always perceived as good) to the church is seen in the church's own embarrassment over the local congregation. Whether it is because the church has unthinkingly adopted the skepticism of the culture concerning any instance of the particular, or whether it is because, in its forgetting of Jesus Christ, it has sought to make God so utterly transcendent that no community of faith could ever be taken seriously as sharing in Christ the divine life, or whether it has merely adopted the style of corporate America and viewed the congregation as a local branch of some national office, there has grown up an almost patronizing attitude to the worshipping community within the church itself. That precisely there we are engrafted into the body of Christ, are baptized, fed, and commune with God and find each other; that precisely there saints are formed in the world, saints whose lives alone change the world; that precisely there life together becomes life in Christ lived in his service, all of that is found to be secondary to the more important task of becoming useful to the world. Not surprisingly, even the church, especially the church, is scandalized by its own particularity and must forever receive it as a gift from the hand of the particular God who meets us in Jesus Christ. That God surprises us with such a gift is the happy message which the act of preaching is given to unfold.

And it is a message we *can* preach. Perhaps the most singular aspect of Jesus' ministry was his refusal to work alone. He gave tasks to his disciples, some large and some small, none unimportant. So many of his stories concern landlords or masters who go into a far country and entrust their land or their work to others, indeed, to nothing more than their servants. In a way, the most singular aspect of the gospel itself is the fact that this story is put into the hands of the church. Jesus, as Lesslie Newbigin reminds us, unlike Mohammed, wrote no gospel.[12] His story was told by others from the beginning, just as it is today. How shameless of God, careless really, to leave this story in our hands! Yet he does and seems to think the story is strong enough to capture our hands and our hearts and get itself told through us, even in spite of us.

Why, then, should we belittle this task? Is it beneath us? Is our modesty about the work of the church and its "powerlessness" in the world really so modest, or does it conceal, rather, a hopelessness about what God is able to do with us, a despair which suspects that, in fact, we are beyond redemption? Is there not a curious kind of pride that is ashamed of the gospel, fearful of being identified with something that may reveal how weak and pitiable our own faith is? We think we know that, and so we are modest. But, in fact, such modesty is not the humility of grace but, rather, a pride that wants to avoid grace, that wants to assert itself precisely to keep from being judged and redeemed. There is nothing modest about such an effort at all; it conceals a yearning to be the judge and ruler of one's self.

But forgiveness is imperialistic in its claims and never more so than in its insistence that only in Jesus Christ are we known. One learns humility in his school, just as one learns confidence there, too. For, as the gospel insists, he is not ashamed of us and, in forgiving us, calls us to quite specific tasks. Indeed, that is the nature of his generosity; he gives us work to do, work that identifies us as his. The God and Father of Jesus Christ, who saves by grace alone, does not work alone, but his grace is such that we are for the first time given a sense of his purpose, given, in fact, something to do with our lives that counts. That is also the gift of preaching, that it contradicts our deep-seated despair and hopelessness by witnessing to the importance of our own work, the gospel significance of our own lives, the grace of being called to give what we have.

*   *   *   *   *

The gospel, when it is preached, is not only a word of faith that challenges the powers of our world, not only a word of hope that gives us direction and work to do, but it is also a word of love which reveals to us both the mystery and the laughter of the divine comedy.

There is, on the face of it, nothing more absurd than a preacher trying to point to something quite beyond his comprehension, something as mysterious as grace. But, in fact, that absurdity does not constitute the preacher's chief dilemma. For the great mystery of grace is precisely its comprehensibility. What puts the preacher into a predicament is not the fact that God is so far beyond us that none of us can understand him, but, rather, the fact, the alarming fact, that God has come so close to us we can see with startling clarity the mysterious depth of his love. In Jesus Christ, God reveals himself, not something less, not something tricky or intricate or complex (which, however, with the help of some *gnosis*, we can then demystify), but himself. The blinding clarity of such a gift is, of course, what scandalizes us; it comes in human flesh, being born in something less than impressive surroundings, dying in rather questionable circumstances. We see all of that. But what is given in all of that is not something hard to understand but, rather, something that is hard to accept.

What we would prefer is to determine in advance that God is a mystery and then demystify him according to our lights. As long as we keep God so mysteriously transcendent, we can then free ourselves for the important work of developing his usefulness. But what explodes this contrivance is the clarity of God's self-revelation. He gives us himself. He comes as the man Jesus Christ and refuses to be separated from his story. To be sure, there is a mystery about this Jesus. The Pharisees, his family, his own disciples often *do not understand him*, but their lack of understanding, like our own, stems not from what Jesus refuses to say or what he refuses to disclose but, rather, from what he does say and from what he does do. "Love your enemies." "Do not be anxious." "He who loses his life shall find it." "Father, forgive them." The mystery of these words is a mystery that Jesus unfolds as a mystery, a mystery precisely where we thought there was none, but which we now see, in his self-giving, to be a mystery quite beyond our grasp. Here, as in so many other places, Jesus teaches us what is mysterious, so that the mystery becomes one of his own giving.

Only such a mystery is able to resist our "explanations." That is what surprises most of all and what constitutes the true joy and freedom of preaching, preaching that is, which is entirely useless in "explaining" this gift and, therefore, entirely free to proclaim it. It is such freedom and such joy, not our "explanations," that are truly subversive of the world's self-importance. "He who sits in the heavens laughs" at the vain conspiracies and plots of nations and kings. Preaching the gospel helps us hear that laughter and, indeed, faithfully echo its joy.

And yet, precisely such a mystery is placed in our hands. The gift of preaching and its mysterious power stems from this reality, viz., that Jesus Christ places himself in our hands, as bread and wine, as word and worship. The people who come are right to expect to be fed; they are right to be impatient with "explanations"; they are right to wait for nothing less than God. That is why preaching is the happiest of callings and why it is entirely useless for anything else except its quite particular task of speaking God, the God who speaks his word in Jesus Christ and identifies himself as the Father of this Son who in the Holy Spirit gives us this particular word of good cheer to say.

NOTES

1. Flannery O'Connor, *The Complete Stories*. (New York: Farrar, Straus and Giroux, 1971), pp. 375 f.

2. *Ibid.* p. 360.

3. Ralph Wood, *The Comedy of Redemption,* (Notre Dame, Indiana: University of Notre Dame Press, 1988), p. 122.

4. Flannery O'Connor, *op. cit.* p. 377.

5. Cf. the end of the story where the water-stained shape of a bird on the ceiling of Asbury's room "descends" implacably "emblazoned in ice instead of fire." p. 383.

6. Gerhard Forde, "Naming the One Who Is Above Us" in *Speaking the Christian God,* ed. by Alvin Kimmel, Jr., (Grand Rapids, Michigan: Eerdmans, 1992), p. 111.

7. *Ibid.* p. 111.

8. Sally Fitzgerald, ed., *The Habit of Being,* (New York: Vintage Books, 1979), p. 88.

9. *Ibid.* p. 479.

10. Cf. Lesslie Newbigin, *The Gospel in a Pluralist Society,* (Grand Rapids, Michigan: William B. Eerdmans, 1989), especially his chapter on "The Logic of Election" pp. 80-88.

11. *Ibid.,* p. 160.

12. *Ibid.,* p. 97.

A Sermon

"Not Refusing the Gift"

Preached on Sunday Morning, August 23, 1992, at
First Presbyterian Church
Kerrville, Texas

Let us pray: What are we to make of a gospel that is a gift, O Lord? A project we could understand, a duty we could perform, but a gift? A gift we can only receive. So open up our clenched fists and make of them receiving hands, ready to grasp the gift put in our midst in Jesus Christ our Lord. In his name we pray. Amen

> *"See that you do not refuse him who is speaking. . ."* Hebrews 12:25

Whenever I go to a professional baseball game these days, which, sadly, is not as often as I would like, I no longer take my glove. Maybe it's because I'm an adult now, or supposed to be anyway, or maybe it's because I would prove an embarrassment to my children or friends who might go to the game with me. Or maybe, in fact, it is a sign of hopelessness. You see, when I was a boy, I would always take my glove when my father and I would watch the Houston Buffs play. You had to have a glove in case a foul ball came screaming at you and you would have to stab at it with your hands. The fact that we usually sat in the right field bleachers and would go a whole game without even hearing a loud foul bothered me not a whit. Like

Linus, I believed. And I was ready. Surely one night it would come and I would pick it off with my J.C. Higgins "Bob Feller" model glove.

Well, the foul ball never came. I remember my father's purchasing a ball from the Buffs at Christmas time and giving it to me for a present, but, as nice as that was, it wasn't the same as catching one. So I grew up and before long quit taking my glove to the game. I was older and wiser and perhaps also a bit sadder.

Sometime later, when I was a teenager, I was with my family in Richmond, Virginia, and received an invitation from some friends to go to a ballgame between the Richmond Cavaliers and the Rochester Red Wings. It was late in the summer, and neither team was in the American Association pennant race, and there were not very many folks in the stands. Our seats were near the left-field bullpen, and as Richmond began scoring runs, we could almost touch the relief pitchers from Rochester as they began warming up. Seeing them up close rather spoiled my image of ballplayers as young, lithe, Adonises strolling the green fields of play. These guys looked old, broken down, and maybe a little bit hung over. In any case, they seemed none too optimistic. One of them sat on the bench near me spitting tobacco on the foul line. On an impulse, I asked him where he was from. "Hattiesburg, Mississippi," he replied. He had been up with the Orioles for a cup of coffee, but clearly he was on the downhill side of his career and was now playing out the string in triple A. The next year he would be out of baseball altogether. At the end of the line, in a meaningless game, he had time for this kid who was peppering him with questions. Finally the call came for him to warm up, and I watched him stretch old and aching muscles and limber up by throwing a few soft pitches to the catcher. Gradually his speed increased until I could hear the catcher's mitt explode with a pop. He was sweating now and clearly in a groove. The manager called time and walked slowly to the mound, and then I saw him motion to my friend from Hattiesburg. As he grabbed for his warm-up jacket and started for the mound, I yelled out, "Good luck!"

He stopped and turned to me, and for a moment I thought I had said something wrong. But then he smiled and took the ball out of his glove and tossed it over the rail to me. "Here, kid," he said, "this is for you." I caught it and held on to it as if it were gold. A gift. It was a gift I no longer expected but now had received. I covered it with my hands and smelled its wonderful aroma of leather and grass and sweat. And all the way home I cradled the gift in my arms.

Such moments are remembered in part because they are so rare, but also because they seem to find us rather than our finding them. And there is no explaining them, no rationale for them; they come, and we are not asked to explain them but simply receive them. "Here, kid; this is for you." As simple as that.

And as difficult. For not all gifts come stitched in leather to be tossed about so easily. In fact, often such gifts can shatter us. We go so many times to the ballpark without getting a foul ball that soon we stop taking our gloves; we go to worship so many Sundays hoping for something to eat, and soon we start leaving our appetites at home. And yet, there is something a bit ridiculous about going to a ballgame to get a foul ball, as if that were the point of the game. We miss the game that is before our eyes if all we are interested in is foul balls, just as we miss the gospel, the joy that is set before us in worship, if all we insist upon is "getting something out of it." More often than not, worship, when it happens, is what gets into us or, better, what, unexpectedly gets hold of us, and shows us a world, a gift we had never seen. Jesus parables are full of stories about people who are eager to "get something out of life," only to be surprised and even disappointed when they are presented with life as a gift, something they had not bargained for. An elder brother works all his life to earn the right to claim what belongs to him and cannot stand to be told that it is his only as a gift from the father. The laborers work in the vineyard, coming at all hours of the day, and are shocked to hear that the wages are the same, that the last receive the same as the first, as if what was being paid was not wages but a gift. Peter declines to let Jesus wash his feet, knowing

better than Jesus that such work is beneath him, and is
shocked to discover that such work is a gift, without which
one has no part in Jesus at all.

Time after time in the New Testament, the disciples,
rather than figuring out the gift, blunder upon it in a bur-
lesque of grace. A Mary Magdalene has long since left her
glove at home; she has come to the garden to preserve a
corpse only to find the risen Lord who calls her by name.
Or the two disciples on the road to Emmaus carefully explain to the rather dull stranger why it is no longer necessary to bring your glove to the game anymore. "The game's
over," they tell him. "Wait till next year." And then, among
the peanuts, popcorn and crackerjacks, they stumble upon
the gift itself, burning their hearts as he reveals himself in
brokenness.

It's as if the gospel is about people who cannot get
away from this gift. It finds them: in a far country or in
their own backyard. That, in any case, is what the letter to
the Hebrews thinks. The gospel, the author says, is not
"darkness and gloom," something which, like castor oil,
tastes awful but is supposed to be good for you. The problem is not how we can get folk to swallow the stuff, much
less how we can disguise its taste. Try as we might, and we
try awfully hard, the gospel cannot be turned into medicine
or a project or an explanation that we somehow must make
attractive in order to get people to listen to it. The pessi-
mists are, the author of Hebrews thinks, ironically right:
there is no escaping, no exit. The wages are the same. The
elder brother and the younger brother both have to deal
with the forgiveness of the Father; they cannot escape, but
what they cannot escape is not the bad taste of something
that is good for them but, rather, a gift. They cannot escape
grace. Indeed, they are surprised by grace.

That is what the world is up against, Hebrews suggests, in its opposition to God: not a god whose demands
silence us into submission or anger but that One who finds
us in our deepest despair and hurt and tosses us a ball, a
life, a hope and says, "Here, kid; this is for you. It's a gift."

I have never been to Wrigley Field but I am told

that when opponents hit home runs there, the fans, loyal to
their beloved Cubbies, throw the balls back onto the field.
They refuse to accept the gift. It is, I suppose, a rich person
indeed who can throw back such a gift, even from a tainted
source, but perhaps loyalty has its own rewards. One hopes
so; there have been few enough for Cub fans. But I wonder
if we are not like those fans more often than not. A gift
drops into our lap, and because we were no longer looking
for it, we ignore it or toss it back. "See that you do not refuse him . . . ." Hebrews reminds us, for this gift can no
more be escaped than death itself. In fact, it comes to us
where we least expect it: in the death of Jesus Christ, something we constantly try to throw back on the field, as if we
could escape it. Not what we wanted; not what we expected; not what we ordered. "Let him deliver him who delights
in him." "Get this thing out of here so that it can close out
of town." How could such a death be a gift to me? How can
death be anything but bad news?

In one of her aphorisms, Simone Weil reminds us
that the one indispensable requirement for eternity is death.
It comes in no other way.

Cecil Barrilleaux understood that, though he could
never have explained it. The gospel, I am convinced, can
never be sought; it can only be found, and just as we sometimes receive a gift, so there are times when all we can do
is give a gift. Cecil was a project, nothing more, nothing
less. Retarded, he lived in the state school, a recipient of
good care, if somewhat official love. Not at our request but
at theirs, Cecil began coming to worship. The school wanted to put him in a social setting before ultimately releasing
him altogether. Cecil could talk but only with great difficulty. His face was disfigured, his steps slow and awkward; he
was not a handsome sight. We complimented ourselves on
our tolerance and generosity in taking on Cecil and socializing him in worship and refraining from commenting on
his obvious disabilities. We were good, we thought, for Cecil. He was our project, and we were hard at work with
him. And the strange thing was that Cecil seemed to enjoy
it. He loved worship. He couldn't sing a lick, couldn't read,

couldn't respond, couldn't do anything but sit there with his brown suit on, wearing a silly smile. But he loved it, loved putting his suit on and coming to church.

And all went well. Our project was moving right along until Cecil the project became, in a terrifying way, Cecil the gift. One day he was diagnosed with a particularly virulent form of cancer, losing first an arm and later his life. Toward the end, I went to visit him in John Sealy Hospital in Galveston. I found his room, and when I walked in, he smiled the biggest, ugliest, happiest grin I ever saw. And gave me a hug with his one good arm. We talked for awhile, and I asked him if he were frightened. He looked down at the bed and nodded his head. This was not how things were supposed to be, I thought. We were just working on a project, not dealing with life and death. We hadn't signed on for that. We were just socializing, right? Just playing church? But now in that room there was fear, palpable fear, and longing and hurt. Was Jesus Christ available there, too? In that mammoth, state-run facility, in that antiseptic and characterless room, was there also a bit of grace? The words came to me: "If I make my bed in Sheol, thou art there." Well, if this wasn't Sheol, it was a reasonable facsimile. Yet I had no words of grace and felt as frightened and as useless as Cecil. That is the way, I think, God brings us to the cross, that is, by revealing to us our uselessness and inviting us to share in the helplessness of another. Finally, Cecil looked up at me and said he wanted to go home; he wanted to put on his suit and go to church. I smiled at him and said that he would be going home soon, I hoped, and for him to keep his suit ready. He replied that he had it in the hospital, and then he showed it to me, neatly pressed and hanging in his closet, the one thing in the room that said "Cecil." The effort had tired him, and he lay down after that, very near tears now. "You'll be coming home soon," I said, "and you'll wear your new suit. But you don't have a tie, Cecil." And he looked at me, and I took off my tie and folded it on his pillow and put it beside his head. "Here, Cecil; this is for you." He smiled and for a moment was no longer afraid.

At Cecil's funeral, the sanctuary was filled. We thought that Cecil was a project, something we were sup- posed to work on but found out instead that he was a gift we were invited to receive. The words, "Here, kid; this is for you," or "Here, Cecil; this is for you," are not quite the same, but they are close enough to remind us of how God gives gifts to us: Take, eat; this is my body which is for you; this do in remembrance of me. "See that you do not re- fuse him who speaks to you . . . But let us be grateful for receiving a kingdom that cannot be shaken." A kingdom that cannot even be shaken by our refusal to receive it as a gift but has a way of making us stumble into grace so that, dying, we truly begin to live. "Here, kid; this is for you. It's a gift." Indeed it is.